MW00466839

continued

Restorative Literacies

Creating a Community of Care in Schools

Deborah L. Wolter

Foreword by H. Richard Milner IV

TEACHERS COLLEGE PRESS

TEACHERS COLLEGE | COLUMBIA UNIVERSITY
NEW YORK AND LONDON

Graduate School

Bethelhem, PA   www.iirp.edu

Published simultaneously by Teachers College Press,® 1234 Amsterdam Avenue, New York, NY 10027 and the IIRP Graduate School, 531 Main Street, Bethlehem, PA 18018.

Front cover photo by FatCamera / iStock by Getty Images.

Library of Congress Cataloging-in-Publication Data

Names: Wolter, Deborah L., author.
Title: Restorative literacies : creating a community of care in schools / Deborah L. Wolter ; foreword by H. Richard Milner IV.
Description: New York, NY : Teachers College Press, 2021. | Series: Language and literacy series | Includes bibliographical references and index.
Identifiers: LCCN 2020051139 (print) | LCCN 2020051140 (ebook) | ISBN 9780807765210 (hardcover) | ISBN 9780807765203 (paperback) | ISBN 9780807779491 (ebook)
Subjects: LCSH: Reading—Remedial teaching—United States. | Children with social disabilities—Education—United States. | Community and school—United States. | Restorative justice—United States.
Classification: LCC LB1050.5 .W656 2021 (print) | LCC LB1050.5 (ebook) | DDC 372.43—dc23
LC record available at https://lccn.loc.gov/2020051139
LC ebook record available at https://lccn.loc.gov/2020051140

ISBN 978-0-8077-6520-3 (paper)
ISBN 978-0-8077-6521-0 (hardcover)
ISBN 978-0-8077-7949-1 (ebook)

Printed on acid-free paper
Manufactured in the United States of America

Contents

Foreword

Increasingly, I hear educators talking about restorative practices, restorative discipline, and, in fewer cases, restorative justice. The language of restoration is encouraging to me as someone who has attempted to disrupt traditional mindsets, attitudes, dispositions, ideas, and related practices of "classroom management" in classrooms, schools, and districts. While I am encouraged by these discursive shifts—from managing and controlling bodies to restoring relationships—I simultaneously am concerned by the underdeveloped conceptual knowledge of some educators in what could be called a restorative movement in education. Similar to conversations about culturally relevant and culturally responsive pedagogy, restorative (justice) practices require deep, robust knowledge and understanding for ideal process implementation and potential outcomes. In other words, how do we support educators in their journey to practice what they are coming to talk about as an alternative to "classroom management" practices that exclude, punish, and dehumanize students?

Restorative Literacies is an excellent tool to help educators, both newer and experienced, build the necessary conceptual knowledge and consequently the belief systems that profoundly impact their practices. At a time of immense cultural and racial disconnects; pervasive inequitable structures, institutions, and systems; and deeply ingrained uncertainty inside and outside of education, this book offers a refreshing perspective on the power of story in cultivating emancipatory, restorative, and transformative contexts of learning, teaching, and development. Wolter reminds us of the plurality of literacy, beyond simply reading and writing. Literacies of restoration propel educators to identify the many assets of their students, allow and expect young people to question and critique, build bridges between themselves (as educators) and their students, and acknowledge that pursuing justice is not destination work (Milner, 2020).

Through eight stories of restorative literacies, Wolter skillfully teaches as she reflects and builds knowledge. Drawing from her rich experiences cultivating a love of reading among her students and studying the practices of other educators and students, she advances in this book a provocative set of examples about centering the voice and stories of people in our quest to humanize and reimage how we care for, about, and with others. Importantly,

Wolter shepherds readers through her own learning and development as an educator committed to getting better for her students. She refuses to let her students down or fail, and they co-create restorative circles of healing as they listen to one another, build respect and trust, identify who has been harmed, and chart a path forward.

Indeed, restoration demands that educators understand the social, affective, behavioral, cognitive, intellectual, and relational needs of their students. It advances the social and the relational as precursors and companions to emphases on academics. In short, educators understand that when they are relationally disconnected from their students, academic success is more challenging. Restoration requires educators themselves to reflect on their own role in the conflicts and challenges between themselves and their students, rather than placing conflicting onuses on students. Moreover, restoration demands a focus on harm; that is, who has harmed whom? Identifying harm and those who have been harmed allows those in the sociopolitical context to journey forward toward healing. Harm and hurt make it difficult to build and sustain the kinds of relationships needed in order to traverse through challenging times and situations. Indeed, it is difficult to maximize teaching and learning when relationships are not a central element of the classroom. Perhaps most important, restoration has the potential to assist educators in a necessary fight to end the school-to-prison pipeline, where pushout practices have been designed to control students and prevent them from reaching their capacity (Milner et al., 2018). These pushout practices dramatically begin for Black students in the very early years of their educational experiences and have a potentially significant impact on their learning and development in schools and consequently on their experiences in society.

A welcome addition to the literature on equity, *Restorative Literacies* is an invitation to be hopeful during a time when many people feel hopeless. The shift to restore and heal rather than marginalize and ostracize is not an easy endeavor. Similar to living, learning, and teaching, the stories shared in this book are challenging and at times even frustrating. However, Wolter necessarily and poignantly walks readers through nuance and complexity with clarity and confidence. During these times of civil and civic unrest, this is the book we need in education. Educators committed to building their knowledge and understanding about the potential of restorative literacies ought to "circle up" around this book.

—H. Richard Milner IV,
Cornelius Vanderbilt Chair of Education, Vanderbilt University

Everyone Has a Story

As an author telling the following stories, it is my responsibility to share my own story—who I am, my perspectives, and the lens that I look through. Educators who work with students from cultures, languages, and abilities different than their own must be incredibly reflective. Not only must educators be reflective of the students they work with and the multiple kinds of literacies (Kirkland, 2014; Lazar et al., 2012), digital literacies (Morrell et al., 2013), and unfamiliar genres (Fleischer & Andrew-Vaughan, 2009) that are part of these students' lives, but educators also must be aware of their own ethnocentrism, of the kinds of books and other material they personally read, and of what their priorities and motives are for teaching language, linguistics, and literacy. I am White. I communicate in English. I grew up and continue to live and work in an area rich with diversity and resources. I have always had food on the table and a bed to sleep in. But I am deaf, totally deaf, in both ears. I lipread and speak. And read and write. I was born in 1962, long before laws were passed to protect my educational rights, but I was lucky to receive an excellent and inclusive education in a progressive public school system. While I have had my share of confronting assumptions, judgment, and discrimination, I don't pretend to know the experiences of others who are, by race or linguistics, historically and currently oppressed. Of course, characteristics of race and linguistics certainly should not be seen as medical conditions like mine, but I suspect that the resulting experiences of microaggression, marginalization, and discrimination are similar for all of us who are the "other" in an educational system inherently designed for White, middle- to upper-class, English-speaking, able-bodied norms. The implications of the above reflection of myself—who I am—are crucial to recognizing that I view other people and their literacies through my own lens.

Just as I do, all other educators carry lenses too. Ignorance, prejudice, color-blindness, projection, confusion, and defensiveness exist in all of us in some form or another at one time or another. People are all bound to err as we move across multiple intercultural and interlingual boundaries. Yet listening, a skill that is often passive, unquestioned, and superficial (Paul & Elder, 2006), is crucial for acknowledging and responding compassionately to anger, frustration, and even silence about literacies. As a long-time teacher consultant, my focus was on the individualized growth of my students—students in special education, in Title I, in response to intervention efforts, and those who were English language learners. However, in my current role as a literacy consultant, I have come to see that educators and administrators also need restorative care in expanding their concepts of literacies beyond basic surface skills and standards.

WHOSE STORIES GET TOLD?

Some stories are heard, but many are not. Too often, "we believe the one who has the power. He is the one who gets to write the story." So we must ask, "Whose story are we missing?" (Gyasi, 2016, p. 226). Restorative literacies begin with stories and re-storying about cognitive and metacognitive processes, identities, diversity, tolerance, inclusiveness, community, and literacies. Restorative literacies merge restorative justice with literacies, building healthy relationships among readers, texts, authors, and educators. Stories also help pinpoint the underlying cultural, linguistic, economic, political, and dis/ableist impacts on surface skills such as decoding, fluency, vocabulary, and comprehension. Restorative literacies adopt the plural *literacies*, as opposed to *literacy*, in that there are multiple forms of literacies beyond what it means to read and write as a basic and functional ability (Barton, 2017; Lazar et al., 2012). Restorative literacies is an approach to building and strengthening positive relationships among readers' backgrounds and perspectives, as well as their variable skills, proficiencies, and fluencies; the multiple texts readers encounter; and the authors of such texts through an intentional system of response, repair, and restoration in an educational setting.

Throughout this book, eight stories, as representative but compelling examples of restorative literacies, provide a deeper understanding of the complex relationship among cognition, metacognition, identity, behavior in schools, and literacies. All people have basic human needs, including celebration, integrity, interdependence, play, spiritual communion, physical nurturance, and autonomy to choose and fulfill our dreams, goals, and values (Rosenberg, 2015). Stories help people empathize, find connection, and even cherish one another, especially in culturally and linguistically diverse communities. And stories can help people embrace and sustain linguistic, literate, and cultural pluralism as part of the democratic project of schooling (Paris, 2012). Even though events and outcomes in stories may be unique to each individual or situation, feelings and needs that are universal to all of us emerge when stories are told or read. Stories are necessary even in the field of education and literacies, so that teachers and administrators can begin to blur the line between objectivity and compassion both between themselves and all of their students, and among one another.

Teaching is incredibly demanding work. Our nation is now in a national climate of hard conversations about our diversity, limited resources, education, and work ethics. Conversations about equity and privilege are constantly at the forefront, particularly in news media and on social networking sites. Teachers, as a collective group, must be strong and well-organized in the face of state standards, high-stakes testing, and limited funding, but at the same time, they are in a fragile and bewildering state of needing to acknowledge—while teaching reading, writing, and literacies—the individual experiences of poverty, adverse childhood experiences and trauma, gun violence, race, immigration, nationalism, and gender and sexuality among their students.

Woven throughout each chapter of this book, for illustrative purposes, are actual narratives from elementary and secondary schools. The names and specific identifying information in these stories have been changed to protect the privacy of the individuals. However, there are other students and educators across our nation's school systems who have similar experiences. The individuals in these stories are not alone.

As teachers and administrators read the stories in this book, they are encouraged to select and visualize one or two of their most difficult-to-reach students, or perhaps their most difficult-to-teach class; picture the students' faces; wonder about their life experiences—both positive and traumatic experiences, their experiences and barriers at school, the literacies in their lives—and consider how to fully listen and respond to both their cognitive and social views of literacies. In other words, educators are urged to "read" robust stories, with character development and multiple plot lines, that contain more than just a superficial view of the cognitive processes of reading and writing. As the stories throughout this book will illustrate, the significance and the implications of those stories will emerge. Most likely, the lessons on restorative literacies from their students' stories will benefit the educators and schools, as opposed to lessons to be instructed directly to the students themselves.

CHAPTER OVERVIEW

After an overview on restorative literacies in Chapter 1, readers of this book may begin by noticing the stories that need to be heard. Not all stories are told outwardly. Many are told in insidious or radical ways, such as through a narrative of silence, behaviors, disengagement, deficit language, race, and the systemic structure of schools. In order to listen well, educators first must notice the language of our students beyond spoken words.

We will meet Alec in Chapter 2, who, after his mother died in an accident, asked why he did not read like his peer, Ellie. Because his teacher noticed an opportunity for Alec to share his story, his educational trajectory took a new direction. This chapter shares how educators can notice and listen for the languages that communicate the needs of our students, other educators, and the community. Once educators notice the language of need, we can begin the process of compassionate listening (Rosenberg, 2015).

Compassionate listening, described in Chapter 3, is a conscious process of ensuring that all involved are fully heard, a skill that requires removing assumptions, judgment, and bias. In this chapter, we will meet Olivia, a 5th-grader, and her entire educational team in the throes of contentious mediation about Olivia's individualized education plan. When people peruse libraries, bookstores, or online catalogs, they are inherently evaluating books—often by their covers, tables of contents, and maybe a few other pages—to decide whether they would like to read a particular book. Keeping cultural values and background knowledge in mind, people check the topic, genre, illustrations or graphs, text structures, complexity of the words and sentences, and other features of the books. People admittedly are *judging* each and every book that is pulled off the shelves. But people, like Olivia and others who are different from ourselves, should not be approached this way. Compassionate listening requires fresh, cold, or sight reading, terms used in education or theaters describing when a person reads a text, script, musical notes, or lyrics without prior exposure or rehearsal. In compassionate listening, the mind is a blank slate and is fully open to learning information, concepts, and feelings.

This book about restorative literacies is structured around the concept of how restorative practices help to reduce crime, violence, and bullying, and to restore relationships, repair harm, improve human behavior, strengthen civil society, and develop effective leadership and sustainability (Wachtel, 2013). Thinking about crime, violence, and bullying forces educators to also think about an expanded view of literacy, as discussed in Chapter 4. Some students, and even many of their parents, have adverse experiences with "school-like" literacy, and their responses may result in intense emotions and behaviors. Some immigrants and refugees have escaped difficult conditions in their home countries only to face bewildering monocultural and monolingual practices in schools. In addition to bringing adverse experiences to schools, some students may suffer further confusion, trauma, and exclusionary practices while at school due to inflexible disciplinary policies and a lack of support in meeting curricular standards. In this chapter, we will meet Diego, who was juggling multiple languages and language variations but still was happily trying to make meaning, comprehend, and learn new words while reading. However, Diego was identified by his teacher as a "struggling" or "low" reader due to his test scores. Instead of a referral to special education, there are restorative practices that take would a positive approach to increasing Diego's literacies, such as expanding the literary canon, minding gaps, increasing metacognitive and metalinguistic awareness, developing vocabulary, and tackling unfamiliar genres.

A key component of restorative practices involves restoring relationships. Chapter 5 notes that educators must restore relationships not only among students, educators, and the community, but also among students and the literacies surrounding them. Ms. Morgan, an elementary/middle school principal, found herself in an intense controversy among her students' parents over how her school should teach reading and writing. Some parents were dogmatic that phonics must be taught in an explicit, sequential, and prescribed manner. Other parents were concerned about the "drill and kill" method of teaching reading, decrying that their children wouldn't want to come to school. Ms. Morgan and all of her teachers were also under pressure from both administrators and stakeholders to close the achievement gap in their school. In the midst of all of the public scrutiny, Ms. Morgan wanted to bring back the access to books, motivation, engagement, choice, voluminous reading, love of literacies, and, yes, reading strategies that included phonics instruction. Through the use of restorative practices and a newly hired literacy coach, Ms. Morgan began to build restorative literacies in which all of the students in her school started to thrive.

In the process of restoring relationships, we must repair the harm done to students over definitions of what it means to be literate. Literacy and "being educated" are not interchangeable (Taylor & Dorsey-Gaines, 1988). In Chapter 6, we will meet Ms. Walker, who was teaching a "tough" intervention literacy class of 8th-graders, most of whom were assessed to be reading at 2nd- or 3rd-grade level and were misbehaving. After trying out several remedial reading programs, as well as various behavior modification methods, with no success, Ms. Walker turned to restorative circles and had positive success toward building relationships with her students and repairing harm and literacies.

When educators want to improve human behavior, as well as view "struggling" readers and writers in a more positive light, they must strengthen their students' decisionmaking and agentic learning. Chapter 7 points out that all people need ownership of their identity as readers, writers, speakers, listeners, and beings capable of reflection and understanding. In Chapter 7, we will meet Lamar, a student who particularly resisted writing activities and confronted "expectations" with vehemence. Lamar had his own way of doing things and needed to be heard. We also will meet Trevor, who diligently complied with anything that was expected of him and copied as much as he could (such as from the whiteboard, mentor books, and other student work) rather than come up with his own words. In this chapter, we see how restorative literacies practices in a workshop model can bring about a deeper inclusion, a shift from doing *to* or *for* to doing *with*, a step from curriculum coverage to inquiry, and a move from passivity to student agency so that all students can thrive.

In restorative literacies, students, educators, and community members can develop leadership and personal, spiritual, ethical, ecological, educational, and political sustainability in a literate society. In Chapter 8, we will meet Aaron, a spirited and opinionated 10th-grader who deeply cared about what was right and wrong in schools. As Aaron was becoming more aware and vocal about racial inequity and social justice, he also was finding himself in more trouble in school. Restorative literacies practices can recognize Aaron's potential leadership and full use of literacies by a shift toward sharing power and a new collaboration, so that literacies are made sustainable for all students in his school.

Finally, Chapter 9 illustrates how educators can strengthen civil society by reducing apathy and disengagement from multiple kinds of literacies. We will meet Jayden, also a 10th-grader, in this chapter. Jayden found himself accused of plagiarism, a concept that he was never taught as he had moved from a highly impoverished inner-city school district to a predominantly affluent school. He thought he was honoring other people's works by including their words in his written pieces, but he had no idea how to cite them properly. Restorative literacies assume that all stories matter, decenters Whiteness, and builds readers' identities, rather than utilizing an unjustified and punitive approach to accusations, such as plagiarism.

There are thousands of stories like these across our country, stories of children, educators, and administrators. Stories of loss and desire. Of dismay. Of exasperation, frustration, and anger. Stories of fear and resistance. Of compliance too. And stories of intense pressure. But convincing people to change their minds about other people is challenging, for it is really the process of convincing them to change their tribe. If people abandon their beliefs, they run the risk of losing their social ties, community, and worldview. Therefore, the way to change people's minds is to develop friendships with them, integrate them into your tribe, and bring them into your circle so that they can adjust their beliefs without the risk of being socially abandoned (Clear, 2019). To change minds effectively, people make particular use of two tools: the stories that they tell and the lives that they lead. The "resonance" that exists—or doesn't—between those stories and those lives has telltale importance as a lever of change (Gardner, 2006).

Both students and educators experience harm in schools: students in facing a dehumanizing focus on standards and compliance, and educators in feeling devalued, receiving low pay, and having strained relationships with administrators. One of the reasons it is challenging to create restorative justice in schools is because it is difficult to determine who has caused harm, who has experienced harm, and whose needs should be addressed (Winn, 2018). Stories overlap and confuse, so educators may strain to answer: Who does the story belong to? But individual stories are born out of systems. Educators do not want to "target" or "fix" the storyteller, but want to hear how systems can be repaired, or navigated, so that literacies are restorative. In the chapters that follow, educators will hear the many stories in our schools and communities and can begin to see how to use literacies as a medium for restorative care.

Acknowledgments

All of us have stories we tell ourselves about ourselves. And we have stories that other people tell about us. For most people, there is a disconnect between their own stories and other people's stories. For some people, however, this disconnect is significant and can result in misunderstandings, microaggression, marginalization, and discrimination. People, from the very young to the very old, desire to be heard. And fully heard with empathy, connection, and restoration.

It takes a village to raise humans, readers, writers, and books like this one. To numerous colleagues, families, and their children who shared their stories, some in a frank manner, thank you for reflecting with me on how people are storied and re-storied.

Thank you to Emily Spangler at Teachers College Press and Craig Adamson, John Bailie, Linda Kligman, Zeau Modig, and Margaret Murray at the International Institute for Restorative Practices, who knew this book needed to be written. They supported me through one of the hardest times in my personal life with understanding, patience, and encouragement.

And thank you to all who saw this book through publication: Adee Braun for her keen editing, Karl Nyberg for his production editing, and Emily Freyer as publicist. Books are not made without you.

And Kara, this is for you. For we both learned how to listen.

CHAPTER 1

What Are Restorative Literacies?

Restorative. *Restorative* is a word that implies that something, perhaps people's health, strength, or well-being, was initially out of sorts and needed to be restored. People feel rejuvenated when they've had rest, a long run, a massage, a glass of wine, or had their woes heard. Restorative practice has become a catchword in criminal justice, social work, counseling, organizational management, and education. While many children learn to read and write easily, breeze through school, and head off to college or careers, seemingly resilient in dealing with their challenges along the way, a significant number seem to struggle to read and write in a proficient, fluent, and engaging manner. Very few children succeed against all odds. But when people highlight those few against-all-odds stories, the message is that all it takes to succeed is grit and resilience and willpower (Gerald, 2018). Too often, when there is a focus on successful outliers, systemic and structural injustices are ignored, carrying the message that if students don't succeed in school, it's the students' fault. Therefore, restorative practice is not about restoring an individual student's literacy; it is about a community of care (Wachtel, 2013).

Restorative literacies is an approach to building and strengthening positive relationships among readers' backgrounds and perspectives, as well as their variable skills, proficiencies, and fluencies; the multiple texts readers encounter; and the authors of such texts through an intentional system of response, repair, and restoration in an educational setting. Restorative literacies, often treated grammatically as a plural but defined as a singular concept, is embraced within a pluralistic society. Restorative literacies reconcile cultural, linguistic, economic, political, and dis/ableist views of literacies with cognitive and metacognitive processes of reading proficiency, fluency, and comprehension, and writing encoding and effectiveness. The reality of literacies is complex, and restorative literacies can keep education policy from hiding behind this complexity and focusing solely on phonics or a simple "science of reading" that involves only decoding ability and equates language comprehension with reading comprehension. A declaration of the simplicity of literacy, namely, a focus on the "basics" of reading and writing, places policymakers and educators in danger of being seen as authoritarian, prescriptivist, exclusive, and even racist and ableist.

Restorative literacies, morphed from restorative justice and restorative practice, is about restoration of systems—systems of parents, teachers, principals, and administrators—so that *all* people, not just students, experience racially, culturally, linguistically, economically, ably, and politically responsive, authentic, and engaging dialogue and learning opportunities involving multiple forms of literacies. And restorative literacies is for educators, especially those coming from dominant populations, too. It is needed by educators to allow them a safe place to widen their definition of literacy beyond simply decoding, fluency, and comprehension (A. Johnson, 2019) and toward an expanded definition that includes social concepts of literacies. *All* people, not just students and not just those who are different from the mainstream, need tools to navigate the complex issues of identity, diversity, prejudice, and power in their daily lives so that they may learn, thrive, and succeed in a diverse society (Derman-Sparks & Edwards, 2010). What better way is there than to use the mediums of literacies widely available in our modern society?

RESPONSE, REPAIR, AND RESTORATION

Ethnocentrism, color- (and other identity) blindness, meritocracy, deficit mindsets, and ableism have been bandied about as possible roots of gaps, disproportionality, and marginalization in education. While U.S. educators, most of whom are White, English-speaking, female, able-bodied, and middle class, may be fully aware of what might be insidious social and political contributions to opportunity and achievement gaps in schools, they are not entirely sure how they can begin to make positive change for individual students in their classrooms. Although teachers certainly do not mean to harm individual students, and even though some students bring adverse experiences from homes and communities to schools, recognizing that some students experience additional harm at school is crucial. Such harm can occur through the use of socially acceptable covert segregation (such as tracking and special education classrooms), zero-tolerance disciplinary policies, and standard curriculum that does not adequately bridge, connect, and expand students' schema to academic literacy. By starting with noticing the language of stories and with compassionate listening, educators can respond, repair, and restore relationships with literacies through actively altering, navigating, or even disrupting the status quo in the systems and structures of our schools.

Building positive relationships in teaching and learning communities is crucial. Too many students pass through school feeling unknown, uncared for, unsupported, and disengaged (T. Howard, 2020). Even if a single educator is not responsible for a single student's educational history per se, response, repair, and restoration can begin to change the student's trajectory from a poor to a positive outcome. Many students need not only *response*, as in culturally responsive teaching, but also *repair* of the sense of direct or indirect harm they experienced and continue to carry. Repairing can orient toward a solution or a reparation of an original problem. Since some students have confronted countless instances of belittlement of their difficult experiences, educators must note that it is the students themselves who personally feel harmed, and perhaps shamed, regardless of whether other people are willing, or not willing, to acknowledge that harm and shame. Often, response and repair alone are not enough. Students need *restoration* of their sense of community belonging and capable literacies practices. All three terms are used throughout this book to ensure a fully inclusive space for restorative literacies.

HOW RESTORATIVE JUSTICE INFORMS RESTORATIVE LITERACIES

The concept of restorative literacies is influenced by concepts of restorative justice. Restorative justice is a positive shift from punitive approaches to criminal justice, especially as compared with processing in the traditional juvenile court (Bouffard et al., 2017). There are three approaches to criminal justice: (1) retributive justice (punishment), (2) distributive justice (therapeutic treatment of offenders), and (3) restorative justice (restitution) (Van Ness & Strong, 2010). Similarly, literacy instruction and educational attainment in schools are viewed by some students as a distressing and punishing endeavor where teachers, in turn, may see the need for detention (retributive justice) or therapeutic remedial reading programs (distributive justice). Thus, restorative literacies (restitution) can closely model restorative justice approaches.

Zehr (1990) noted that when crime is seen as a violation of the law, punishment is determined by the state according to systemic rules. A different lens is created when crime is seen as a violation of people and relationships. Even if an offender and a victim had no previous relationship, a crime creates a relationship. Through this lens, restorative justice creates obligations to make things right. The restorative justice process involves the victims, the offenders, their families and friends, and the community in the search for repair, reconciliation, and reassurance. Zehr added that while crime represents an injury to the victim, it also may involve injury to the offender. Much crime grows out of injury, for many offenders experienced abuse themselves and do harm in part because of harm done to them. Likewise, restorative literacies in schools can repair and reconcile relationships between readers and texts and their authors.

While the terms *restorative justice* and *restorative practices* appear to be used interchangeably in the literature, Wachtel (2013) distinguishes between restorative justice and restorative practices. Restorative justice is a subset of restorative practices, and is *reactive*, a response to crime or other wrongdoing. Restorative practices, on the other hand, are processes that proactively build relationships and communities to *prevent* conflict and wrongdoing. Restorative justice in schools should not be just about crime between offenders and victims, but restorative practices should conceptualize essential questions about the historical and embedded power relations between teachers and students and between schools and homes (McCluskey et al., 2008). Restorative practices, at any age or grade, provide means for promoting diversity, tolerance, and inclusiveness through responsible community practice and peaceful expression of conflict and reconciliation (United Nations, 2006). Restorative practices reduce further violence, shame, stigmatization, and alienation of both the offender and the victim (Wachtel, 2013). Addressing feelings of violence, shame, stigmatization, and alienation as a result of struggles with proficiency in reading and effectiveness in writing is the ultimate goal of restorative literacies.

Despite many well-intentioned approaches and reforms over several decades, many students are *still* not considered as achieving in reading and writing at expected rates. The achievement gap, and its companion, disproportionality, are thoroughly documented and recognized in educational research and policy as well as in general news media. Many states are now moving from the use of zero-tolerance policies to restorative practices as a critical step toward the goal of reducing exclusionary practices. Restorative literacies, which combines both cognitive and social views of literacies, in practice draws upon theoretical studies and practices in reading, writing, literacy, social–emotional learning, diversity, culturally responsive teaching, restorative practices, and restorative justice.

CONSIDERING THE COMMUNITY

Of relevance to a discussion about restorative literacies in this book is the need to restore community. It is suggested that a government's role is to establish and preserve a just order, whereas a community's role is to build and preserve a just peace. When community peace is sufficient, there will be little need for order. Likewise, when there is little peace, more order is needed (Van Ness, 2012). This dualism between government and community becomes apparent to educators who try to address deviant behaviors in classrooms, but do not fully realize that, quite like fostering community peace, they may need to restore teaching with multiple forms of literacies promoting understanding, empathy, and connection.

Definitions of community, inclusiveness, and literacies may conflict with individuality, differences, and diversity, especially when people consider "other" people as "outsiders." Most people define community as people with whom they are intimately close, their families, their circle of friends, and perhaps their places of worship and workplaces. People in a community may share similar races, economic means, and values. But building community (and building literacies) is about expanding the boundaries beyond traditional communities to include an ever-widening awareness of humanity (Boyes-Watson, 2005). And often, this expansion occurs in public school systems having a highly diverse population of youth. Furthermore, expansion can occur in myriads of literacies.

Books and other reading material can be a viable source of expanding our worldview. Using the metaphor of mirrors, windows, and sliding glass doors, Bishop (1990) noted that when children cannot find themselves mirrored and reflected in books, or when they find that their image is distorted, negative, or laughable, they learn that they are devalued in the society they are part of. Children from dominant populations have plenty of mirrors, but lack windows in books for viewing and understanding others. People of all ages need sliding glass doors in books to step through and enter a real or imagined world—one that includes respectful dialogue and empathy.

Although people may try to celebrate diversity and condemn division in their communities, people are too often ignorant of the underlying role of authoritarianism and culture. Political dissent, moral deviance, and intolerance of racial diversity, or any kind of "difference-ism," are all driven primarily by authoritarianism as a result of a fundamental and overwhelming desire to establish and defend some collective order of oneness and sameness (Stenner, 2005). According to Gelfand (2018), behavior depends largely on whether we live in a *tight* or *loose* culture. Tight cultures have strong social norms and little tolerance for deviance, whereas loose cultures have weak social norms and are highly permissive. People are rule makers or rule breakers. This tight–loose difference can emerge among countries, across states, and within organizations. The tight–loose differences can become apparent in smaller groups, such as in neighborhoods, schools, sports teams, and clubs, as well. And tight–loose differences certainly manifest in literacies too, in terms of what books and other texts are acceptable or banned, or what items, memes, or commentaries are shared on social media. Even very young children learn social norms from their immediate environment, and they also shape and enforce these norms. But when children cross cultural boundaries, particularly when they come to school, they can find themselves bewildered and, in some cases, in trouble.

RELATIONSHIPS AMONG IDENTITY, BEHAVIOR, AND LITERACIES

Identity, behavior, and literacy are closely tied. Schools face a number of challenging, disruptive, and antisocial behaviors that seem to get in the way of reading and writing instruction. Undesired behavior may include horseplay, rule violation, disruptiveness, class cutting, cursing, bullying, sexual harassment, refusal, defiance, fighting, or vandalism (Osher et al., 2010). Some behaviors also may appear hostile, rebellious, aggressive, threatening, or strange. Students who bear labels such as emotionally disturbed, mentally ill, or behaviorally disordered, or otherwise appear abnormal, tend to be considered fundamentally different, possibly dangerous, and even illiterate. The competitive and conformist nature of schooling actually may exacerbate students' original problems, particularly when these problems are positioned in such a way as to make it seem necessary to remove and control them (Stoughton, 2006).

Experienced teachers have always noted that classroom management and students' lack of motivation for learning are two of their greatest problems in schools. However, pedagogy characterized as having constant teacher direction in reading and writing skills (such as imparting information, making assignments, asking questions and expecting correct answers, monitoring seatwork, marking papers, grading tests, settling disputes, and punishing misbehavior), and commanding student compliance, seethes with passive resentment that sometimes bubbles up into overt resistance (Haberman, 1991). A vicious downward cycle of the poor relationship between discipline and teaching continues when educators fail to acknowledge and address the overly directive and authoritarian type of teaching commonly found in urban schools (Haberman, 2010), as opposed to teaching that fosters authentic, engaging, collaborative, and reflective inquiry, comparisons, analyses, syntheses, evaluations, and generalizations—in other words, teaching that fosters cognitive conversations and social interactions with *literacies*.

Osher and colleagues (2010) offer three approaches that show promise in improving school discipline practices and student behavior: an ecological approach (increasing the strength and the quality of classroom activities, including the use of authentic and purposeful literacies), schoolwide positive behavioral supports (defining, teaching, and acknowledging a common set of positive norms), and social–emotional learning (self-awareness, self-management, social awareness, relationship skills, and responsible decision-making). Losen and Martinez (2013) noted that restorative practices hold promises for school discipline as well. A central goal of restorative practices is to change the mindset of people by helping them gain a greater respect for individuals in their community, including themselves, and more accountability to the community at large. Not only is there repair to the victims who have been harmed, but the needs of the offenders also are addressed. The International Institute for Restorative Practices (2018) noted that all humans are hardwired to connect. Embracing an expanded view of literacies is another excellent medium for human connection. Restorative justice models bring together perpetrators and victims of misconduct, whereas restorative literacies bring together books, digital media, and other forms of texts; their authors; and readers. While a community, inside and outside schools, is being made whole, at the same time literacies are viable tools for bridging understanding, empathy, and compassion.

Restorative literacies depend on personal relationships using feedback, scaffolding, and collaboration, not on testing data alone. When miscues in reading and writing are expected and embraced, feedback on the current and expected levels of performance, and the metacognitive and metalinguistic actions needed to close the gap, has a powerful impact on student learning (Fisher et al., 2016). Furthermore, grouping students by abilities (or benchmark levels), within classes or between classes, has negligible impact on learning. Even though ability grouping is a traditional and common practice in schools, it most often leads to disruption, ostracization, and tracking (Fisher et al., 2016). But when there is collaborative instruction, practice, and feedback, in dynamic and flexible groups, the outcomes can be compelling, not only for the children but for educators who are open to learning more deeply about the literacies in their communities.

HUMANITY, JUSTICE, AND A NATURAL SENSE OF CURIOSITY

Children come with a natural sense of curiosity, humanity, and justice. They ask *what*, *why*, and *how* seemingly all the time. They explore and delve into things big and small, muddy and all. If an adult tells a child *not* to do something, invariably the child will get mightily curious and go right to it. Curious learners go deep and they go wide; they take risks, try things out, and allow themselves to be distracted. Curiosity can be unruly and a threat to established order. But all the while that they are besotted with curiosity, children are gathering cultural information—what is right and what is acceptable versus what is wrong and what is unacceptable (Leslie, 2014).

Our nation is currently in a climate of difficult discussions about injustice, educational and economic inequity, diversity, and nationalism. The dynamics of institutional and systemic advantages and disadvantages are deeply rooted in history (Derman-Sparks & Edwards, 2010). "We see people willing to go along with the way things are, even when the way things are deny people their right to freedom and full humanity" (Torres, 2018). But children have a humane and innate sense of justice and can show us where to go with conversations about important issues. After all, children of all ages are not immune from society's hard conversations. They overhear opinions of adults, are bombarded by media blasting from every corner of their daily environment, and engage with social networks. And children regularly make frank commentaries that can awe their adult listeners, causing the adults to stop and remark to themselves or to others around them, "out of the mouths of babes." At the same time, children learn prejudice from prejudice—not from learning about human diversity. It is not human differences that undermine children's development, but, rather, unfair, hurtful treatment based on those differences (Derman-Sparks & Edwards, 2010).

Unfortunately, in schools and in literacy instruction, children dutifully answer questions rather than wonder and ask questions. Too often, schools are designed to prepare children to take their places in the social order without questioning and challenging that order. Compliance is emphasized, or else the "troublemakers" may be subject to referrals for intervention or special education, pathologized testing, disabling labels, hallway work, medication, remediation, detention, suspension, or expulsion (Shalaby, 2017). Furthermore, students are taught that anger is impolite and improper. But anger can be a strength, a survival mechanism, a confirmation of existence, a way to be heard. At the same time, students who are called "scholars" also may be oppressed. Often, the "scholars" are students who are talented test-takers, not critical thinkers. Thus, neither population is free. Only when both the oppressed and oppressor carry the courage of independent thought can systems of oppression fall (Wojtowicz, 2018).

Systems of oppression manifest in English language arts classrooms of all grades. For children who may be struggling with reading and writing, their days of "literacy" may be filled with watered-down tasks, worksheets, and low-level books that require very little reading. Their literacy instruction may target specific skill deficits, and they may endure round-robin reading that publicly exposes their errors and dysfluency (Allington, 2013). School or academic literacy seldom reflects the literacy practices of historically oppressed groups and is characterized by narrow views of what counts as literate performance and who counts as a literate person (Kirkland, 2014). However, using literature, writing, and the English classroom as sites of justice, restoration, and peacemaking should not be a revolutionary concept, either for youth who have experienced the school/prison nexus, or for youth who have had a relatively successful academic trajectory (Winn, 2013). What would happen if adults saw all students as *explorers* of language, linguistics, and literacies, rather than as students having sets of surface skills to be mastered in a lockstep fashion? How can educators acknowledge and make connections with the language, linguistics, and literacies already occurring in children's homes and communities? In restorative literacies, the ability to listen will not make teaching easier; it will not take the painful parts away. But listening can bring children back (Minor, 2019).

CHILDREN'S RIGHTS TO READ

What would happen if people started to see children as "small humans" and less like "little kids" (Torres, 2018)? The determination of legal rights for children, as apart from human rights, invariably has rested on adults' perspectives and decisions. The idea of *children's* entitlement to certain provisions and protective measures or mechanisms could not exist without the existence of *childhood* as a distinct, conceptual category (Strauss & Powell, 2015). Ontology deals with the nature of being, of what is, such as "what is a child?" or "what is childhood?" There are many ontological positions that may be taken, such as that children are biologically immature humans who are developing; that they are an oppressed minority group; that they are in need of guidance, education, care, and support; or that they are inherently vulnerable and dependent upon adults for protection. Other ontological positions can view children as competent agents who actively contribute to our world, who have their own culture that is very different from that of adults, and who are experts in their own lives (M. Gallagher, 2009). Rights and protections for children are based on multiple ontological positions. For example, the United Nations Convention on the Rights of the Child focuses on civil, political, economic, social, health, and cultural protections for children based on their vulnerability in our communities (United Nations, 1989).

Language and linguistic rights are the individual or collective human and civil rights to use one's own language both in private and in public. The United Nations Declaration on Rights of Persons Belonging to National or Ethnic, Religious and Linguistic Minorities (1992) states that persons belonging to national or ethnic, religious, and linguistic minorities have the right to enjoy their own culture, to profess and practice their own religion, and to use their own language, in private and in public, freely and without interference or any form of discrimination. However, it is very difficult to make a case for language rights in education, particularly in our increasingly globalized world. Advocacy for a dominant language, such as English, in schools as a means of global interchange and social mobility must be balanced with the rightful use of local languages, which may entrench social, cultural, and political isolationism, as well as disadvantage students socioeconomically. Thus, acceptance for bilingualism and English learner programs is potentially fragile and easily dismantled in schools (May, 2014).

Children also are seen as having the right to read. The International Literacy Association (2018) developed a position statement on children's rights to read as an issue of social justice and equity. Reading enriches the life of an individual personally, socially, and culturally. Furthermore, the ability to read represents the difference between inclusion in and exclusion from society. Some of the basic rights to read include the right of individuals to access texts in print and digital formats, the right to choose what they read, and the right to share what they learned through reading by collaborating with others locally and globally. Most important, children have the right to benefit from the financial and material resources of governments, agencies, and organizations that provide reading and reading instruction. A declaration of children's rights to read is pointed toward building more support for urban school districts having fewer resources and more unqualified teachers and unsafe conditions.

Not only do children have the right to read, but they also have the right to read books of their choosing. Certainly, parents can provide guidance to their own children, but allowing the imposition of their values upon a wider culture stymies our inquiry about, understanding of, and empathy for other people. The American Library Association (2019) states that library policies and procedures that effectively deny minors equal and equitable access to all library resources available to other users violate intellectual freedom and the Library Bill of Rights. The association opposes all attempts to restrict access based on the age of library users, including limiting the selection and development of library resources simply because minors will have access to them. The National Council of Teachers of English (2018) further asserts that one of the foundations of a democratic society is the individual's right to read and the individual's right to freely choose what they would like to read. When educators reject works that may be "emotionally inappropriate" for children, they are adhering to the traditional view that children's literature should avoid controversial topics (Ringel, 2016). Some books and periodicals have been criticized as objectionable for being too modern or overly realistic or containing "ungrammatical" English, bad language, or suggestive material. When these books are attacked for being "controversial," it suggests that for some people the purpose of education is not the investigation of ideas, but rather the indoctrination of a certain set of beliefs and standards. This results in an environment where many students are "educated" in a system that is hostile to critical inquiry and dialogue (National Council of Teachers of English, 2018). Certainly, care must be taken when selecting and recommending engaging material, but not at the cost of marginalizing populations of students.

Young people care very much and yearn to make a difference in their world. Instead of being seen as innately rebellious, they should be viewed as people with profound and important ideas (J. Fox, 2008). In restorative literacies, educators certainly can continue to foster surface reading and writing skills, deeper comprehension processes, and personal choice and voice, but they also must add restorative practices that fully embrace students and communities in their ontological rights, language rights, and rights to read.

RELATIONSHIPS AMONG RESPONSIVE TEACHING, SUSTAINABILITY, AND RESTORATIVE PRACTICES

Culturally sustaining pedagogies and responsive practices in schools are crucial for both reaching all students and moving toward fostering authentic and engaging literacies. The term *culturally sustaining* requires that pedagogies be more than just *responsive* to the cultural experiences and practices of children. It requires that schools *sustain* the cultural and linguistic competence of their communities while simultaneously offering access to dominant cultural competence (Paris, 2012). Ethnocentrism—people's tendency to see other cultures and languages from the perspectives of their own cultures and languages—occurs in all people. But too often, U.S. schools are operated and taught from a dominantly White, middle-class, English-speaking, and able-bodied perspective. Culturally sustaining pedagogy is not about simply being responsive to the "needs" of individual students, and neither are restorative practices. Both culturally sustaining pedagogy and restorative practices are not solely about "curing" students, raising test scores, or closing disciplinary or achievement gaps.

Both culturally sustaining pedagogy and restorative practices are about listening to the voices of children *and* educators. The goal of both practices is to foster polyvocal classrooms (Morrell, 2018) and create a community that treasures freedom of speech (both orally and in print), and also teaches responsibility for the quality of the discussions (Noddings & Brooks, 2016). The intersection of home and school experiences—both in terms of realities and hardships and in terms of positive relationships and personal experiences—should inform our curriculum, instruction, and assessment (Milner, 2015).

Schools are confronting a vicious downward cycle of disproportionality and covert segregation. While some school factors result in disproportionality and covert segregation, there are multitudes of outside factors as well, including poverty, housing, and gentrification (Mordechay & Orfield, 2017). Overt forms of racial segregation, such as the so-called "separate but equal" facilities in employment, medicine, housing, transportation, and, prior to the Supreme Court's landmark *Brown v. Board of Education* decision, education, have given way to more covert forms of racial segregation in special education or other forms of resource rooms. Disability, instead of race, has become a socially accepted, even normalized, category of marginalization for students of color (Ferri & Connor, 2005). The pattern of within-school segregation based on achievement or perceived ability has persisted for decades without much public outcry, even though millions of students, teachers, and administrators observe it at school every day, and it has been well-documented by education researchers (Tyson, 2013). School communities also should accept and value people with medically identified disabilities as people who have cultural and linguistic identities in their own right, and should recognize them not simply as a population to which something unfortunate has happened (Garland-Thomson, 2016).

No student should check their linguistic, literate, and cultural identities at the doors of our schools. Unfortunately, the wide varieties of languages and literacies in our communities, and people's abilities in them, are viewed, positioned, and even tested against White, middle-class, English-speaking, and able-bodied norms. Therefore, schools as institutions tend to operate on deficit approaches that attempt to eradicate the linguistic, literate, and cultural practices that many students of color bring from their homes and communities, and to replace them with what are viewed as superior practices (Paris, 2012). Instead, schools must strive toward pluralism in practice, not just in theory. A pluralistic society has *energetic engagement* with diversity, not simply a climate of tolerance toward diversity (Eck, 2006). Pluralism requires both within-group cultural practices and common, across-group practices in order for a global society to thrive and remain vibrant (Paris, 2012).

For example, English is a primary language in our nation and often is noted to be a global language in newspapers, magazines, television, and other mass media. The reality, however, is that there are nearly 7,000 living languages in the world, but despite the extent of language diversity, only a small number of the world's languages are used as mediums of instruction (Wiley et al., 2014). In addition, there are variations in English, ranging from the Boston or Brooklyn accent, to the Southern drawl, to the Yooper dialect, within the United States. And most people know that there are variations in our discourse; we speak English differently in different situations, such as in the workplace, at the local pub, or with young children. Furthermore, written discourse does not always match our spoken language. Many texts are written in a standardized form of English, but others contain stylistic features associated with creative writing or occupational groups such as lawyers or journalists (Crystal, 2003).

A majority of children around the world attend schools where there is a difference between the language or variety of language spoken at home and the language instruction in school (Wiley et al., 2014). Values of pluralism may be a shared ideal, but too often they are not championed in the reality of people's daily lives. Throughout U.S. history, while racism and language discrimination have been closely aligned, linguistic assimilation has been championed as a means for societal assimilation (Wiley, 2014). It doesn't mean that educators need to learn multiple languages or literacies per se—an impossibility given the number of languages and language variations spoken among students in our school systems. But in order to coexist in multiethnic and multilingual communities, educators must open their minds and hearts to cherish and uphold our diversity. And we need to teach students how to do the same, while accepting and bridging the connections they make between their cultural and lingual identities and the dominant forms of literacies used for educational and economic purposes.

A responsive society is needed, and there is no better place to start than by exploring literacies in our classrooms among future generations, especially in the current social and political climate involving Black Lives Matter, immigrants and Dreamers, Islamophobia, nationalism, income inequity, and LGBTQ+ rights. Milner (2018) remarked that it is an *ethical* imperative, not simply an academic imperative, to stay focused on cultural, educational, and organizational transformation in addressing institutional and systemic issues of race and poverty. But as a classroom, school, or district strives toward culturally sustaining pedagogies in practice, restorative practices may be needed to fully get there, not only for individual children, but also for teachers, mentors, administrators, families, and community members. There is no better way for pluralism to flourish than through exposure to a wide range of texts, fiction and nonfiction books, mass media, and even social networking sites. Although this book is about restorative literacies, proficiency, and fluency in reading; effectiveness in writing; *and* identities as readers and writers, it can be co-seated with larger school or districtwide initiatives and agents for change—or, at least, as a place to start.

RESTORATIVE LITERACIES

It is not enough to just tell students that they are capable of learning to read and write. Schools must consciously provide the conditions and opportunities for students to experience their own power for success (Wojtowicz, 2018). However, a clear definition of restorative justice is elusive and is further complicated by the numerous components within programs and practices (between three and fourteen have been proposed) and philosophies (up to seven principles or values) (Song & Swearer, 2016). Zehr (2015), considered the "grandfather" of restorative justice, constructed restorative justice on three pillars: addressing the harms and related needs, holding offenders accountable to put right those harms, and involving victims, offenders, and the community in this process. The United Nations developed a lengthy list containing features of restorative justice programs, such as a flexible response to the circumstances of the crime, an approach that can be an alternative or an addition to traditional criminal justice processes and sanctions, a response that respects the dignity and equality of each person, or recognition of the role of the community as a prime site for preventing and responding to social disorder. The International Institute for Restorative Practice, with particular focus on preventative community practices, noted that restorative practices are not limited to formal processes but can include a range of informal responses, such as affective statements to small impromptu conferences to restorative circles (Wachtel, 2013).

Similarly, a tenet of restorative literacies is the recognition that reading is a complex process. Reading and writing are not "instinctive" like language (Pinker, 2003), but must be taught and practiced in a manner that is responsive and restorative. Restorative literacies is not prescriptive or dogmatic to a particular program or model. The basic premise of restorative literacies is that educators learn *with* their students, not teach *to* or provide *for* their students. It is an open-minded participatory learning process for all people. Restorative literacies is about the cognitive processes of reading and writing as well as about embracing the social views of literacies. Restorative literacies require educators to be incredibly reflective of their ethnocentrism and the diversity surrounding them.

Restorative literacies merge research in literacy with restorative justice. There are plenty of books, journal articles, and websites available for educators and other stakeholders on education policy, multiple literacies, choice and voice in classrooms and libraries, reading volume, access, reading strategies, and even responsive literacy, but restorative literacies are not just about "growing readers and writers." It is about repairing harm, restoring relationships, and expanding the concept of "literacies" for some of our most disenfranchised and disengaged students through a model of compassionate listening, community of care, and restorative practice. Restorative literacies build relationships not only among students and educators, but also with texts and their authors, and between students when they write and the authors of texts.

But before educators can start, they must begin to *notice* the opportunities for stories to be told. Stories are important elements in restorative literacies. Without positioning classrooms and schools as neutral and safe spaces for stories to be told and heard, students, teachers, and administrators will be unable to bridge multiple cultural and linguistic forms between homes, communities, and schools to improve and sustain authentic literacies and educational attainment. Valuing time for stories is healing too. Individual stories shed light on experiences and perspectives, which educators can expand on to more fully address individual learning processes, diversity, and even trauma.

CHAPTER 2

Noticing the Language of Stories

Alec looked smitten. As a 5th-grader, Alec seemed to be experiencing his first crush, a puppy love of sorts for Ellie. Alec knew that a special education teacher was at his classroom door, waiting patiently for him to join her for reading. Alec had been struggling with reading and was recently assigned to Ms. Edman's caseload. Ms. Edman had met him only once before. As Alec shuffled backward toward her, he never took his adoring eyes off Ellie, who was slouched on a dark blue beanbag chair, fully engrossed in a book. When Alec was by Ms. Edman's side, he again acknowledged her presence with a tentative wave, still not taking his eyes off Ellie. Alec and Ms. Edman stood side by side, watching Ellie, who was oblivious to them observing her from across the classroom. From what Ms. Edman thought was Alec's perspective, she saw that Ellie had legs dangling over the beanbag chair, with one of her red Keds with white metal eyelets dropped on the rug. Ellie was holding a book close to her face with one hand and continually twisting, with her other hand, the bright yellow laces of her other Keds placed by her side. She had long straight brown hair with a thin purple braid down one side of her head and a face that appeared calm, assured, and confident. After a few moments, Alec shrugged, turned to Ms. Edman and muttered, "Why don't I read like her?"

Here was an opportunity for a story, a story that needed to be noticed and heard. At first, Ms. Edman wasn't planning to say anything about Ellie, fearing that Alec would feel embarrassed by her observation of his adoration of a beautiful girl at the cusp of growing into a young lady. But Alec startled Ms. Edman by asking why he didn't read like Ellie. So Ms. Edman paused again to observe Ellie reading. Ellie was indeed absorbed in a chapter book, proficiently and fluently reading from page to page. Comprehending, visualizing, questioning, and thinking, Ellie was thoroughly engaged in the imaginary world of the book in her hand.

Upon returning to her office with Alec, Ms. Edman asked Alec to share more about what he meant by his comment about not reading like Ellie. Alec set off a litany of the differences between his reading and Ellie's reading. Alec was expected to read out loud to a teacher at a horseshoe-shaped table, but Ellie got to read alone on a beanbag chair. Alec was expected to place his book flat on the table and point to each word as he read, but Ellie was holding her book close to her face. Alec was reading picture books, but Ellie was reading chapter books. Alec was sounding out letters and words, but Ellie was reading whole pages. Alec's reading was always recorded, timed, and corrected, whereas Ellie seemed to be left alone most of the time. Alec even remarked that he was biracial and Ellie was White. Finally looking up at Ms. Edman with exasperation, Alec demanded to know why reading was different for him than for Ellie. And then slouching in his chair, he asked why he was a "bad reader." It occurred to Ms. Edman that a focus had been placed, perhaps over the years and not just in his current classroom, on Alec's cognitive processes for reading—his skills, proficiency, and fluency. Yet the missing link for Alec was his personal, cultural, linguistic, and economic view of his desires and potential growth in literacies.

Alec's mother died in an accident just months before Alec and Ms. Edman met, throwing the whole family into grief and turmoil. He knew his father was grieving, and at the same time struggling to hold his full-time job as a pipefitter and to begin raising four boys, one still an infant, on his own. Feeling the weight of responsibility as the oldest child, Alec said that he wanted to read and to help his three younger brothers learn to read like Ellie. Since his mother died, Alec's father repeatedly reminded him to honor his mother by "doing well in school" and "getting ahead." However, Alec, two of his brothers, and their father, normally used to playing basketball in the neighborhood park while their mother cooked dinner, suddenly had to band together to take care of the baby, cook their meals, keep the house tidy, mow the lawn or the shovel the driveway, and make sure that all homework was done and carefully placed in backpacks. Alec complained that there wasn't even time for watching football games anymore. But Alec wanted to "do right" and wondered just how he was going to learn to read "good and fast" like Ellie. This story is not about his reluctance to join Ms. Edman for his reading session, or about a crush after all, but a different story about a desire to read well. It is not just Alec who needed restorative literacies, but potentially also his teachers, his father, and his brothers.

NOTICING THE LANGUAGE OF STORIES

Stories first need to be noticed before being heard. But stories are not always told at dinner tables, on stages and in films, in media, or through books. Stories are told within the walls of our schools, many in insidious or radical ways. The question is, How well do educators notice the stories that need to be heard, especially the diverse stories that are outside their own knowledge and experiences? Behaviors, disengagement, and even silence all carry unheard stories entrenched in apathy, resentment, and frustration. Educators must explore the idea that students may experience turmoil at school, whether or not they experienced turmoil or trauma in their homes or outside school (A. Johnson, 2019). But some children also experience exploration, exuberance, and joy—strengths that may come across as troublemaking (J. Fox, 2008). Such stories in schools are the proverbial "canaries in the coal mine," for "troublemakers" are the ones educators can learn the most from (Shalaby, 2017). Troublemakers call out the need for educators to listen and listen fully. But first, in restorative literacies, adults must *notice*. The cognitive skills of reading and writing are almost always noticed, but educators also must notice the interrelationship and reciprocity between behaviors and the language surrounding literacies.

The discipline of noticing provides a way of working against the tendency to forget, to be so caught up in our own world that we fail to be sufficiently sensitive to possibilities (Mason, 2002). It seemed that Alec, the student who seemingly had a crush on Ellie, was dragging his feet toward his classroom door for his reading intervention session. While an assumption was made that Alec was in the throes of young love, there could have been other assumptions, assumptions that Ms. Edman avoided making. Alec easily could have been seen as a reluctant, distracted, or defiant reader. But by pausing, noticing, observing, and listening, we found that Alec had a story that needed to be heard. His was a story of loss, desire, and motivation.

When deviance or noncompliance is noticed as *informative*, as an exercise of power and free will, rather than as a *problem*, students are telling educators, loudly, visibly, and memorably, that the arrangements of their schools are harmful to human beings. It is dangerous to exclude these students, to silence their warning. Instead, educators can begin to think about what we can learn from these students, not what to do about them (Shalaby, 2017). Behind every "behavior problem" is a story that gives meaning to that behavior (Gold, 2016). Schools can be hurried, unruly, and stressful places, not only for students but for educators, administrators, and parents as well. But mindfully noticing, listening, and responding to interwoven human stories is an underlying key to restorative literacies.

Listening for Stories Behind Behaviors

Making the time and space to listen is hard, but immensely valuable, work. When the time and space were made for listening to Alec, the underlying truth of Alec's story emerged as one that ordinarily would not have been thought of or entirely heard. Listening is a complex and dynamic process. All people are influenced by both internal and external factors that color their perceptions and subsequent interpretations (Brownell, 2015). Schools and classrooms are bustling places with many students vying for attention at once. Instead of listening fully, educators often insist that students listen: listen to instruction, lectures, and directions; behave and comply; and read and write. However, numerous studies point to "teacher-talk-dominated" classroom experiences of many children, one of which Rowe (2004) eloquently referred to as "the sea of blah." Children are listening to (or tuning out) lectures, long-winded explanations, repeated directions, constant reminders, and voice-overs in announcing and informing all kinds of activities. With good intentions to support Alec for "disciplinary reasons," he was constantly near his talkative teacher—at her horseshoe table for instruction, near her desk for independent work, or by her side during classroom or hallway transitions. However, despite moments of inadvertent inattention as a result of tuning out his teacher to focus on the tasks at hand, it was actually quite admirable how well-behaved he usually was. The paradox is that children learn how to listen by being listened to. And just like adults, children want to share those good feelings by listening to others (Shafir, 2003). Therefore, an inflexible response to misbehavior, such as those practiced in zero-tolerance or "tough-love" environments, is likely to undermine student–teacher relationships, reduce instruction time, lower overall school performance, and harm students' futures (Losen & Martinez, 2013). Alec's teacher admitted to a fear that if she'd "let him loose" in her classroom, Alec would become distracted or otherwise get into mischief of sorts. Therefore, she maintained her watchful focus on Alec without realizing his untold desire to learn to read proficiently like his classmate Ellie. The day-to-day vigilance may feel safer in a busy school environment, but because of it, Alec's story remained unheard. And Alec remained untrusted to take ownership of his learning. Alec persistently retreated into his silence, coasted along, and simply tried to be a good student.

Listening lets educators know the child, individually, culturally, and developmentally; builds a sense of community; makes open-ended questions effectively heard; and helps children become better communicators (Denton, 2013). Instead of insisting that Alec remain close by his teacher for instruction on surface skills, do meaningless worksheets, and read low-level books, restorative literacies bring out stories like Alec's and begin the work of repairing harm and restoring relationships.

Taking the time to listen to students is proactive toward avoiding both difficult behaviors as well as the use of instructional programs or methods that are not well-matched to the needs of individual students. With restorative literacies, Alec was able to explain that he was lucky that he had "easy" worksheets to do, with all the hubbub surrounding his teacher, but he wasn't reading like Ellie. He wanted a turn on the beanbag chair. He wanted to read real books, especially chapter books and graphic novels. He wanted to belong in his community of literacies. After all, Minor (2019) reminds educators that "teaching is dialogue, not monologue" (p. 17). With restorative literacies, "misbehavior" can be greatly reduced when there is mutual conversation and when surface skills are taught through student-chosen, relevant, and engaging content.

HEARING THE LANGUAGE OF SILENCE

Alec wasn't too noisy by nature, but having very little opportunity to be heard, Alec was silent. After finding out from Ms. Edman about Alec's story, his teacher reported that the silence in her classroom was deafening. As a thoughtful and caring teacher, she wondered how many other students in her class were unheard. Even though she couldn't hear stories among her students at first, she began to seek out and listen for more stories in her classroom, among her students' parents, and online. Troublemakers make noise when others are silent (Shalaby, 2017). Alec, as a biracial male, admitted that even though "stuff," such as apathy, defiance, and disruption, happened in school among his Black peers, he still wanted, just as much as every other student in our country, to be safe and especially to be educated. We know that many young Black males lead scarred lives due to oppression and violence. But we must remember that they live many stories beyond narratives of oppression, which in turn shape the ways they read, write, and manage their world of texts (Kirkland, 2013). However, Kirkland remarked that stereotypes rely on silence; "to not tell such stories we add to this silence a face of incredible and willing ignorance that masks dehumanizing discussions of Black males under the veil of (mis)understanding" (p. 9). Alec's teacher came to realize that the color of Alec's skin and the fact that he was a boy, still in 5th grade, influenced her vigilance and control over Alec's daily activities in her classroom. She was, in effect, stereotyping Alec, and in turn this stereotyping was unquestioned throughout the entire school community.

Educators unwittingly tend to be silencers, largely through the need to be in control, politically correct, and physically and emotionally safe. Furthermore, under the weight of following mandates, curriculum, or educational fads, students become data points; they lose their personhood (Minor, 2019). The loudest argument for quiet, an attempt to block out the voices around us, may be a reflection on what otherwise remains in danger of going unheard (Prochnik, 2011). Alec's teacher admitted to her need to control Alec, always keeping him by her side. While silencing is a form of covert oppression toward others who are of diverse races, languages, and abilities, being mindful of children who are shy or introverted is important as well. Alec's teacher ran into this difficulty as she zealously pursued stories in her classroom. While Alec was more than willing to open up about his experiences and perspectives, there were a few students in her class who were unwilling to share much about themselves. Without getting too hung up on exact definitions (there are almost as many definitions of *introvert* and *extrovert* as there are personality psychologists), shyness is the fear of social disapproval or humiliation, while introversion is a preference for environments that are not overstimulating (Cain, 2013). Multiple reasons exist why many children in schools remain mum, but with time, flexibility, and trust, all children can be heard in myriads of ways, through listening, sharing, reading, writing, and reflecting, in environments fostering restorative literacies.

Noticing the Language of Disengagement

Silence does not mean only that one can hear a pin drop in a classroom, but also that student voices are unheard. Ellie was seemingly engaged in her literacy practices, but Alec was simply behaving or attempting to behave. Alec's teacher, like many other teachers, considered poverty, lack of parental education, poor print environments at home, second-language issues, the era of the hurried child, and other (and easier) entertainment options that lure students away from reading as suspects for the decline of reading (K. Gallagher, 2009). But many of the reading practices found in today's classrooms actually are contributing to the death of reading. Many reading difficulties stem from lack of interest in reading, especially when students are relegated to phonetically decodable text that they find nonsensical and boring (Harvey & Ward, 2017). Systematic killing of the love of reading is often exacerbated by the inane, mind-numbing practices found in schools (K. Gallagher, 2009). The different instructional practices in literacy for Alec were made very clear. He complained about having to read at the horseshoe table, with his book flat on the table, and being made to read word-by-word out loud.

Alec's teacher meant well to rein in Alec's behavior in the classroom and to support him in any way she could. She wanted all of her students to learn to read and write. However, she was taking a bottom-up approach in reading instruction for Alec, assuming that a set of surface skills—phonics, sight words, and reading speed—automatically would bring comprehension and motivation. But Alec was in 5th grade. He had already had years of instruction in reading skills. Yet Alec was not a strategic, engaged, and well-practiced reader. At the same time, Alec's teacher took a top-down approach for Ellie in which Ellie honed her skills "naturally" in a literate-rich environment using high-quality children's literature, raising the question of whether Ellie actually was receiving challenging instruction, including criticality, or simply left to her own devices because she was assumed to be a "good" reader.

Educators need to cultivate innate curiosity and capture readers with compelling ideas, artifacts, issues, and generally irresistible content (Harvey & Ward, 2017). This can include not only books, but poetry, memes, photographs with captions, cartoons, graphic novels, and short articles. These kinds of authentic materials can be used to get both Alec and Ellie started on a path of curiosity, criticality, and growth in literacies. Furthermore, students benefit from choosing their own books and often show a desire to read other material of the same or a similar topic or author. Students also benefit from re-reading texts as they sharpen their decoding skills and deepen their comprehension. Student choice is synonymous with student engagement in both reading and writing. Frequent, voluminous book reading builds fluency, stamina, vocabulary, confidence, and comprehension (Atwell, 2015). Instead of seeking workbooks and phonics programs, Alec's teacher needed to flood her classroom with rich and authentic literacy for all of her students, even Alec, and allow room for student voices and choices. However, in restorative literacies, it is not enough to simply hand students interesting books and other texts; it is necessary to intrigue students *and* explicitly teach reading proficiency, fluency, stamina, and deep comprehension in the *context* of their chosen books.

WATCHING FOR DEFICIT LANGUAGE

Students can be silenced and disengaged through either hearing about themselves in deficit language or through systemic and structural ways that place them in deficit situations. Even deficit language must be noticed before we can begin to eliminate the consequences of such language. Schools are obsessed with comparisons, gaps, and weaknesses among students' reading achievement, which in turn leads to diagnoses, labeling, and categorization of students. Too often, labeling and categorization require a diagnosis of some sort to obtain services, necessitating something to be "wrong" in order for schools to pay attention to students. The "disease" versus "normal" split is inaccurate and potentially harmful (Gold, 2016). Far too many children with disabilities, including racial minorities disproportionately identified as having disabilities, are inordinately segregated and insufficiently challenged, reflecting continuing low expectations. Attitudes toward disability have a major impact on the education children receive (Hehir, 2005). If educators are going to remediate weaknesses, they must have an equal commitment to strengths (J. Fox, 2008). And educators must build and strengthen positive relationships between the backgrounds and perspectives, as well as the variable skills, proficiencies, and fluencies, of readers, the multiple texts readers encounter, and the authors of such texts.

Alec previously was diagnosed as having a severe learning disability and was placed for half of his school days in a special education resource room. Both Ms. Edman and his teacher took time to ponder his placement in special education, a placement made when Alec was in 2nd grade. Alec spent 90 minutes a day reviewing 26 letters and 44 phonemes on an online computer program, presumably to help him with decoding skills. Alec also spent 15 minutes a day practicing reading "sight words" on flash cards with an assistant teacher. These flash cards were to help him with quick recognition of words. Finally, Alec spent another 30 minutes working on "repeated reading" exercises to help with his reading fluency. He was to read aloud a phonetically and vocabulary-controlled passage of 100 words, on which he was timed. His time and the number of errors he made would be graphed on a chart. Alec would listen and read the same passage as it was read aloud by an assistant teacher. Then Alec would read the same passage again, attempting to increase his speed and avoid errors. The text would be read three times, each time with the time and number of errors marked on a graph. If Alec reached a success point, the next text would be at a slightly higher level. After all was said and done for the day, Alec was allowed to play word games, do word searches, or do easy crossword puzzles for his remaining time in the resource room. Alec never had opportunities to apply his knowledge of letters, sounds, and words to reading and writing in an authentic and engaging manner. Instead, he was labeled as learning disabled and as one who needed to be closely monitored, as a result of the deficit mindsets of the adults surrounding his literacy. Alec even called himself a "bad reader." Absolutely, both Ms. Edman and Alec's teacher wanted Alec's self-concept as a bad reader to change.

According to Harvey and Ward (2017), we need to think of readers not as struggling but as *striving* readers; moreover, schools need an "intervention on interventions" (p. 39). In order to avoid the pitfalls of response to intervention reading programs, educators must give striving learners the same opportunities as the strongest readers to engage in meaningful literacy (M. Howard, 2009; Wolter, 2017). An inclusive environment fostering restorative literacies, one in which Alec could learn alongside Ellie, can provide strength-based literacy instruction and practice without directly resorting to the use of labels, levels, and isolated and fragmented "reading" programs.

HEARING THE LANGUAGE OF RACE

Hearing the language of race takes courage. Race—and thus racism, in both individual and institutionalized forms, whether acknowledged or unacknowledged—plays a primary role in students' struggle to achieve at high levels (Singleton, 2012). Too often, people who are White pay little attention to the significance of their own racial identity in that they think of themselves simply as "normal" and think that issues of race involve only "other" people. Many White people also perceive themselves as color-blind, so they are unaware of their underlying assumptions about other racial groups. They usually think of racism as the overtly prejudiced behaviors of individuals, without noticing and acknowledging that racism also occurs in an institutionalized system of advantage benefiting Whites in subtle as well as blatant ways (B. D. Tatum, 2017).

Educators often do not discuss issues of race (or language, gender, social class, or abilities) openly and critically in schools. Alec, who was wondering why he was reading differently than Ellie, did note that he was biracial and Ellie was White. Alec's teacher had never discussed race with her colleagues or with students until Ms. Edman brought up Alec's story. Unfortunately, many teachers believe that ignoring race—adopting a color-blind stance—is the best way to overcome its negative power (Southern Poverty Law Center, 2019). For example, in efforts to reverse trends of poor reading outcomes among African American male adolescents, the multiple in-school and out-of-school contexts that they have to negotiate are often ignored when instructional plans are developed or adopted, curricula are selected, or their placement in low-level or remedial courses is examined (A. Tatum, 2008). Even though she was most concerned about the achievement gap in her building and about the Black students who were far below target in their reading and writing development, Alec's teacher unwittingly took a color-blind approach with her class, without seeing the impact of her stereotyping on Alec's opportunities for learning literacies. There are many whispers about race throughout schools, such as Alec's story, but most go unheard.

Race has much more meaning than just the color of people's skin. Educators should refer to race, not "color," because the meanings, messages, results, and consequences of race are physically, socially, legally, and historically situated in power relations by human beings, not by some predetermined set of scientific laws or genetics (Milner, 2015). Additionally, conversations about race are not only about color, but also about Whiteness (Southern Poverty Law Center, 2019). When White educators break the silence about race and racism, they can address their own racism, the racism of other Whites, and the racism embedded in our institutions. Educators can interrupt the White fragility, a state of mind in which even a minimum amount of racial stress becomes intolerable, triggering a range of emotions such as anger, fear, and guilt, and behaviors such as argumentation, silence, and leaving the stress-inducing situation. These behaviors, in turn, function to reinstate White racial equilibrium (DiAngelo, 2011). Instead, educators can begin to build capacity to sustain cross-racial honesty by being willing to tolerate the discomfort associated with an honest appraisal and discussion of our internalized superiority and racial privilege (DiAngelo, 2018).

Teachers' unnoted perception of the literacy and academic abilities of Black students manifests itself in their text selections for these students, the instructional strategies and assessments they use, and the literacy interventions they employ (A. Johnson, 2019). The kinds of texts that Black males, including Alec, as a group encounter in school have been characteristically "dis-abling," lacking a broader perspective and largely ignoring students' local contexts. Instead, there is focus on skill and strategy development, a shift influenced by policy decisions to measure reading output using psychometric instruments (A. W. Tatum, 2006). Alec's previous teachers fell into the status quo predicament of using test results and trying to find a remedial reading program and disciplinary methods that would work for Alec. And Alec, even as a budding reader, was beginning to question the systems and structures of his school, potentially putting himself in a vicious downward cycle of being seen as hostile or rebellious.

The use of the term *achievement gap* allows schools to continue the same type of deficit thinking that created it in the first place. The term permits the identification of Black children as the problem, placing too much blame and emphasis on them as individuals, rather than attending to the disparities in opportunities to learn in the school environments themselves (A. Johnson, 2019; Milner, 2010). The achievement gap in Alec's school was a genuine concern of Alec's teacher, especially in the face of state mandates to close such gaps. She sincerely was trying to close the gap for Alec by monitoring him and working with him on his surface skills. It was distressing for her to see the harm done by the system and structures of the school that she had blindly followed. Restorative literacies calls for a courageous and intentional interruption, which by definition is not passive or complacent (DiAngelo, 2018). A productive shift in literacy takes into account students' four literacy needs—academic, cultural, emotional, and social (A. W. Tatum, 2006). At the same time, educators must understand that responsive and adaptive curriculum practices are not synonymous with low expectations (Milner, 2015). But in order to meet literacy needs in schools having a highly diverse student body, the language of race first must be noticed and fully heard.

LISTENING TO GOALS INSTEAD OF SYSTEMS

Many people, including Alec's teacher, value principles of fairness and equality for people from all walks of life, but how they notice, conceptualize, and practice social justice is challenging. Most people see themselves as acting equally and justly, but in a significantly stratified society it is necessary to go further and explore a critical approach to social justice. Educators must recognize that relationships of unequal social power, even in our schools, constantly are being enacted at both the micro (individual) and macro (structural) levels (Sensoy & DiAngelo, 2017).

School rules are used to create boundaries of acceptability. Children who follow the rules get to be good people, successful students, and fully included members of the class community. Children who fail to follow the rules get flagged, punished, diagnosed, or remediated (Shalaby, 2017). The boundaries of acceptability apply not only to behavior, but also to the ability to read and write on grade level according to school benchmarks and standardized testing. Alec was identified as having a severe learning disability. He was a student who many people assumed was reluctant, distracted, or defiant, especially during literacy instruction. No one questioned how the underlying protective system geared toward students like Alec contributed to his sense of exclusion from literacies in his school community. On the other hand, educators must realize that many students, perhaps Ellie, too, play the game of "school"—behaving well and acing tests—without entirely growing as fully humane and literate beings capable of crossing intercultural and interlingual boundaries.

Alec was seen as having deficits as compared with his peers and in need of a separate program, curriculum, or setting. The provision of special education services that inordinately seek to "cure" disabilities is not only potentially harmful to the child's self-image but may be detrimental to the child's education by pulling them out of important academic education for remedial or therapy purposes (Hehir, 2005). Alec was seen as needing special education for more than half of his instructional day. But while Alec had an unheard story, his individualized education planning (IEP) team were navigating their way through the cumbersome federal and state rules for determining appropriate goals and objectives, psychometrics, accommodations, and ancillary services. Alec's educational team lost sight of authentic and meaningful goals for him. Instead, they began to listen to structural and systemic guidelines for where to place Alec until he got "better" in reading and writing.

There exists an unbalanced opportunity structure that inexorably leads to massive differences in children's overall educational trajectories (Welner & Carter, 2013). Uneven funding in schools, alienating "school reforms," and racism and segregation all converge to threaten students' linguistic rights and literacy potential (Lazar, 2018). Alec was at risk of losing his inclusion as a member of his school community, his participation in a language- and literacy-rich environment, and his chance at educational achievement. In a pluralistic and democratic society, schools must notice and respond to students' actual needs, build on their unique strengths, be culturally responsive, and provide the opportunities necessary to give every student a fair chance at academic success (Welner & Carter, 2013). In restorative literacies, educators can reconcile cultural, linguistic, economic, political, and dis/ableist views of literacies with cognitive and metacognitive processes of reading proficiency, fluency, and comprehension, and writing encoding and effectiveness.

Issues of inequality and inequities in access, achievement, and outcomes for students from racially, culturally, and linguistically diverse backgrounds, with or without disabilities, continue in our schools. However, in efforts to promote equity, people confuse equity with equality through accountability and standardization. Equality, defined as all students receiving the exact same curriculum, material, instructional methods, and disciplinary tactics, does not ensure positive outcomes for all learners. Equity, however, reframes the conversation toward individual students in order to provide resources and supports based on their specific needs. While equality entails equal resources, equity emphasizes equal outcomes. By evaluating the barriers imposed by current mandates for standardized policies and procedures, we can facilitate the discussions, implementation, and focus back to the needs of individual students to provide equity of opportunity for their academic success (Cramer et al., 2018).

Successful U.S. schools having high numbers of students who speak a language other than English, such as Spanish, and students who use Black language patterns, are united in providing a caring, culturally informed, and humanizing pedagogy that recognizes students' knowledge traditions and linguistic assets (Conley, 2018). The startling conclusion is that most school systems are not systems; they are only boundary lines drawn by someone, somewhere (Wheatley, 2010). But schools can move from operating as a historically managed system toward developing into a living system, in which school leaders recognize that our world is complex, integrated, interconnected, reciprocal, and relational, and thus begin to build a culture in which authentic instruction and rich learning can flourish. When educators and school leaders note the reality of the lives and experiences of teachers, children, and their families, they can expand their own knowledge toward understanding the world in which teachers and students live and move. From this perspective, educators can foreground people, like Alec, in the rules and regulations, and move structures and external expectations into a supportive rather than defining position (Mitchell & Sackney, 2016).

Restorative literacies allow educators to listen to goals instead of systems. Alec wanted to be part of his educational community. But most of all, he wanted to be able to read like Ellie. Alec's full inclusion as a viable and contributing member of his classroom community would only increase his reading and writing skills in a manner that would allow him to thrive as well as to be able to support his younger siblings. As a result, Alec was allowed to read on the beanbag chair. He was encouraged to read chapter books that intrigued him, both with his teachers and independently. Alec also was invited to join his classroom's online writing community. Using speech-to-text and word prediction technology, Alec was able to write and share opinion pieces and narratives with his peers. At the same time, his peers, who already had been taught how to use a rubric for reviewing, were able to collaborate with Alec on developing better-quality pieces. In a short time, Alec's time in the resource room as required by his IEP was reduced, and his teachers, peers, and the school community began to see Alec as a reader and writer, instead of a student who must learn skills and be monitored for behavior. Restorative literacies allowed Alec, and even Ellie, to be seen as exploring and growing from where they were, not as having deficits or gaps, or even simply considered "at grade level" and good to go.

Many stories in schools go unnoticed and unheard. Noticing an untold story is the first step to restorative literacies. Educators cannot act if they don't notice an opportunity for a story. Every act of teaching depends on noticing what students are doing and how they are responding, and considering what is being said or done with respect to expectations and criteria.

At the same time, each act of teaching, of caring, or of supporting is also an act of learning about the students, about the situations, and about oneself (Mason, 2002). Yet responses to stories should not involve "curing" or "remediating," but repairing harm and restoring relationships. Behaviors, silence, disengagement, deficit language, race, goals, and systems all carry stories just waiting to be heard. Once educators notice, then they can begin to listen.

CHAPTER 3

Compassionate Listening

Mr. Delaney was dismayed. He walked into an IEP meeting late to find at least 17 people squeezed into a conference room containing a table that seated eight. Extra chairs had been brought in, and people were sitting not only at the table, but along the perimeter of the small room's walls. Mr. Delaney, who taught a combined 5th- and 6th-grade class, recognized his principal and the special education teacher but no one else. He introduced himself to the crowd, stepped back outside and found yet another chair, and squeezed himself in, just behind the closed door. The topic of the discussion that day was Olivia. It was only the 3rd week of September, and all Mr. Delaney knew about Olivia, a 5th-grader, was that she was identified as having a severe learning disability and was in and out of his classroom, spending more than half of her instructional day in a special education room. Whenever Olivia returned to Mr. Delaney's classroom, as she did at several points throughout the school day, she was always bewildered, unsure of what to do next. Olivia was constantly several steps behind her general education peers because she was absent from various activities in her classroom. Mr. Delaney, however, made sure he was there for Olivia, making smooth transitions back to his classroom, explaining what she had missed, or finding her a group to join or materials that she would need. But he saw that Olivia hadn't made new friends yet, appeared reserved, and wasn't reading or writing much in his classroom.

The moment Mr. Delaney walked into the packed conference room, he knew there was a story. And he knew it was not a happy one. He couldn't keep track of all the introductions and was never sure of everyone's role in Olivia's education. In addition to the principal and special education teacher, there were Olivia's parents, their lawyer, an advocate, district administrators, a tutor, a psychologist, a social worker, and various physical, occupational, and speech and language therapists. Throughout the 2-hour meeting, Mr. Delaney listened and came to realize that nothing positive was being said about Olivia or her education. Mr. Delaney heard all kinds of deficit language: Olivia *can't* read, *can't* decode words, and *can't* comprehend paragraphs. Olivia *can't* write, *can't* form her letters in print or cursive, *can't* type, *can't* spell, and *can't* write sentences. And not only that Olivia *won't* try, but that Olivia's prior teachers *couldn't* teach her. And it seemed now that no one *would* try anymore.

Mr. Delaney heard all sorts of exasperation, frustration, and anger from the adults who wrangled about assessment results, goals, and objectives on Olivia's IEP. Mr. Delaney noted to himself that while Olivia might struggle with reading and writing, she also seemed to be an unhappy child. While Olivia's IEP team focused solely on Olivia's skills, proficiency, fluency, and effectiveness in reading and writing, Mr. Delaney knew that regardless of the multiple texts that Olivia would encounter, she needed an intentional system of response, repair, and restoration in her classroom. Olivia was facing a simple dis/ableist view of her reading and writing capabilities rather than a view that considered the cultural, linguistic, economic, and political impacts of her literacies.

Leaning back in his chair, feeling the weight of this meeting on him, Mr. Delaney noticed the literacy coach in the opposite corner of the room. He didn't remember her name or what her role was, but he noticed that she hadn't said a word about Olivia. They looked at each other for a pause, tried not to roll their eyes, and waited patiently for the meeting to end. A week later, when the literacy coach was back in the school building, Mr. Delaney stopped her, asked her to remind him of her role, and wanted to know how to get Olivia back—back with her peers, back to the happy hub-bub of his classroom, and back to her taking full ownership of her reading and writing growth. In the few weeks that he knew Olivia, he saw that she had spunk just waiting to flourish and a great desire to learn. Olivia often carried a book under her arm and would try to read without anyone noticing, and she loved to write on her blog where no one online knew her name. But Mr. Delaney knew he couldn't do it alone. Here we see that restorative literacies are needed not just for Olivia and Mr. Delaney, but for Olivia's entire special education team.

ACTIVE LISTENING AND OBSERVING

Once educators notice a story in need of being heard, they can turn their attention to active listening, response, and action. As Mr. Delaney saw in the contentious meeting about Olivia, listening is a complex and dynamic process. People are constantly influenced by both internal and external factors, such as their organizational roles, attitudes, previous experiences, values, or bias, that color their perceptions and subsequent interpretations (Brownell, 2015). It seemed that everyone at the meeting about Olivia, each person with a different role and perspective, was talking and responding without entirely listening to the other people. And Olivia herself was missing in this conversation. Listening has many facets to its definition. Wolvin and Cohen (2012) provided a useful framework in the form of a five-dimension competency model for listening. Stewart and Arnold (2018) add social listening as another dimension of listening (see Table 3.1). Listening involves more than

Table 3.1. Dimensions of Competency Models for Listening

Dimension	Definition
Cognitive	Understanding how complex the listening process is
Affective	Being aware of emotional barriers we experience in listening
Behavioral	Fully focusing on the speaker
Contextual	Being aware of the setting in which we are listening and using different skills to better listen in different situations
Ethical	Avoiding immediate judgment about messages by listening to arguments and evaluating them
Social listening	Actively processing and attending to, observing, interpreting, and responding to a variety of stimuli through mediated, electronic, and social channels

Source: Wolvin and Cohen (2012) and Stewart and Arnold (2018).

the ability to hear in auditory terms. To listen intentionally, mindfully, and thoughtfully takes much more than just hearing (Wolter, 2018).

According to Milner (2018), schools are experiencing a crisis of self-worth among youth. Valuing the space and time for listening is a significant need for students, educators, families, communities, and society as a whole (Gold, 2016). Olivia's was a story that could have been seen as reluctance, distraction, or defiance. Yet by pausing—and pausing considerably—observing, and listening with an open mindset, we heard a different story. Mr. Delaney, an observant and thoughtful teacher, saw that Olivia was reading on her own and blogging anonymously. And Olivia's story was a story that needed a compassionate response.

Authentic Listening

Minor (2019) points out that authentic listening has three parts: The first act of listening requires us to hear the message coming to us, without judgment, quick solutions, or prescription. Clarifying and paraphrasing may be needed. The second act of authentic listening necessitates deep thinking in order to make sense of what was heard, recognize different value systems, and consider how to respond. The final act of authentic listening involves building bridges, that is, making active and longstanding adjustments in our classrooms, grades, or schools. *Choosing* to listen requires time, commitment, and an investment of energy, and needs to be made a high priority for developing relationships (Brownell, 2015). Listening fully and well to Olivia and other students like her is a paramount step and is probably more than half of the process toward restorative literacies.

Observing

As educators begin to notice and hear the stories behind behaviors, silence, disengagement, deficit mindsets, race, goals, and systems, such as those impacting all of the students, teachers, and administrators portrayed in this book, there must be a willingness to stay present with difficult, intense feelings, while at the same time conveying a feeling of safety (Gold, 2016). Mr. Delaney noticed that people in the contentious meeting about what to do about Olivia offered all kinds of judgments and opinions depending on the perspectives of their respective roles. Only 3 weeks into the school year, he wondered whether some of them had ever worked with Olivia or even met her at all. Mr. Delaney kept hoping to get a better sense of Olivia's own voice in this meeting. But none of that came through. Instead, there was an abundance of federal and state rules, "expert" advice, placement options in special education, and even available remedial reading programs. The culture of deficit discourses, advice, and quick fixes may itself be a barrier to listening and may discourage taking the time to hear a full story (Gold, 2016). This culture of deficit discourse is prevalent in both cognitive and social views of literacies. Working from deficit mindsets is especially damaging when viewed as single stories in either cognitive or social views of literacies as a separate entity.

Striving toward compassionate listening and restorative care requires removing a climate of expertise, insistence, and mandates. Observation can be an important element in compassionate listening and restorative literacies. Observation is the detached and objective process of watching or listening to something or someone carefully as a way of obtaining more information, and from different lenses. But when observation is combined with evaluation or judgment, the likelihood that others will hear the message is decreased. Instead, people are apt to hear criticism and may resist what is being said (Rosenberg, 2015). While it is difficult to make observations, especially of people and their behavior, that are free of judgment, criticism, or other forms of analysis, it is a crucial step toward restorative literacy.

Olivia's IEP containing psychometrics, goals, objectives, accommodations, and programming for her learning disabilities was completely picked apart and every component was disputed. Olivia's special education teacher assumed that consistency and stability, such as using a prescribed and sequential reading program, in Olivia's lessons was most needed at that time. Olivia's social worker made a quick but erroneous judgment that she needed a behavior management program. The psychologist discussed Olivia's mental health and well-being. The principal was worried about Olivia's reading and writing abilities on the basis of her test scores. The lawyer and advocate pointed to Olivia's educational rights to accommodations and special education services. And Olivia's parents—neither of whom had ever set foot inside her classroom or resource room, or had a clear sense of curriculum standards, strands, and scope, and of the wide diversity of instructional needs among the students in those classrooms—offered their individual criticisms of how the school's literacy program should be run.

Absolutely nothing gets done, and neither systemic nor individual progress gets made, when educators, administrators, parents, and community members do not refrain from making quick judgments, criticisms, or evaluations. Withholding judgment is a crucial first step in the process of restorative literacy. And instead of providing an abundance of "expert" advice or mandates, educators must engage in inquiry that allows us to expand our definitions of literacy and literacy instruction (A. Johnson, 2019). This inquiry, as Mr. Delaney and the literacy coach knew, must include observing and listening to our students—who they are, where they are, how they communicate, and how they live, grow, and learn—with an open and positive mindset.

MULTIPLE LENSES

Despite best efforts to listen, when there are multiple people with multiple lenses in a community, even in a school community, views about an issue or a situation may diverge or even clash. The lens through which people view other people may not always be correct, especially if the viewing occurs through a small window of time and space. Mr. Delaney and the literacy coach saw many slices of views on Olivia's abilities and educational trajectory. The recognition of teacher identity, both personal and professional, and how it influences instruction in a diverse student population is paramount. For example, teacher perceptions of the literacy and academic abilities of Black students manifest themselves in teachers' text selections for these students, the instructional strategies and assessments they use, and the literacy interventions they employ (A. Johnson, 2019). Teacher perceptions also can result in early adultification and criminalization of young Black boys between kindergarten and 3rd grade (Wright & Counsell, 2018). Furthermore, despite the reality of our linguistic diversity, people often hold negative attitudes about nonstandardized varieties of English. There are difficult tensions surrounding teachers' desire to honor a student's cultural heritage and their desire for their students to *sound* educated (Hudley & Mallinson, 2015). Due to Olivia's supposed disability, she first was seen through the lens of what she couldn't do, while her nondisabled peers were seen through the lens of what they could do (Ramsey, 2004). Therefore, in restorative literacies, educators must listen keenly not only to others, but to their own inner voices as humans and as educators.

Ethnocentrism

Ethnocentrism is the act of viewing another culture based on preconceptions that are found in the values and standards of one's own culture, especially regarding language, behaviors, customs, and religions. While ethnocentrism in research has been defined in many ways, Bizumic (2019) noted that three major definitions emerged, which educators can be alert to in schools. One definition involves group self-centeredness, in that individuals give strong importance to the particular group they belong to. A second definition involves out-group negativity, such as hostility and contempt toward other groups. And a third definition centers on in-group positivity, in which individuals make positive evaluations of their own groups. Furthermore, there can be a spectrum of higher to lower ethnocentrism within any of these definitions, such as the level of devotion, cohesion, preference, superiority, purity, and exploitation. Although ethnocentrism is found across almost all human groups, it is not found in every person and is less likely to exist in oppressed and lower-status groups (Bizumic, 2019). Insidious sources of ethnocentrism impact literacy instruction when the achievement data of reading and writing among different population groups is the sole focus.

Cultural Relativism

On the other hand, cultural relativism, also a contentious topic within social sciences, is grounded in the idea that other cultures are worthy of as much respect as one's own and should be treated accordingly. Cultural relativism calls for neutral study (for instance, in anthropology studies), greater tolerance, and pluralism (Schaefer, 2008). When educators pause, listen to, and reflect on ethnocentrism and cultural relativism in themselves, among their colleagues, and as entrenched in the system, they can begin to see and bridge cultural gaps instead of simply attempting to remediate achievement gaps in schools. Olivia needed to be seen for who she was, where she was, and where she needed to grow, instead of as a student who is seemingly far below grade level. "Teachers have a tremendous power and potential to narrow the culture and teaching gap that reproduces inequitable student learning outcomes. Their ability to do so resides in their competencies, knowledge, dispositions, and practices, as well as their willingness to deeply understand themselves and their students' cultural identities and backgrounds" (Carey et al., 2018, p. 59).

Color-Blindness

Color-blindness, or other identity blindness, in which an individual makes an intentional effort to "see" people as *people*, not their race, ethnicity, gender, socioeconomic status, or disabilities, invalidates people's experiences and the richness of our diversity. Unfortunately, color- and other identity blindness is inherently a way out of listening. While the color-blind ideology "started out as a well-intended strategy for interrupting racism, in practice it has served to deny the reality of racism and thus hold it in place" (Sensoy & DiAngelo, 2017, p. 131). Visibility, meaning that an individual or group has voice and is heard, is an advantageous and empowering place for that individual or group. Yet visibility can be constraining when individuals or groups are made hypervisible, when differences or failures are magnified, and can result in heightened scrutiny and surveillance. While invisibility and exclusion disadvantage marginalized individuals or groups, they also work in favor of dominant-group members by continuing to reinforce and maintain norms (Settles et al., 2018). Olivia's dis/ability was made hypervisible in the meeting, but Mr. Delaney wanted her back as a viable part of his classroom community.

Multiculturalism

While multiculturalism can create more positive outcomes than color- or identity blindness for interracial interactions, engagement, performance, and detection of discrimination, it also can backfire when there is potential for pigeonholing, caricature, demotivation, and masked discrimination (Plaut et al., 2018). "Even more interesting is how much more important race becomes when boundless energy and effort are placed on suppressing it as a topic for conversation" (Singleton, 2012, p. 39). Color- or identity blindness and misperceived multiculturalism can get in the way of our listening authentically to the voices and stories that need to be heard. Instead of a deafening silence about the issues of race or other differences, listening is an antidote for blindness. Furthermore, color- or identity blindness tends to place emphasis on cognitive processes for reading and writing, and the resultant achievement scores, and tends not to include the impacts of social relationships on literacies.

Listening to ideologies, such as meritocracy, equal opportunity, individuality, and "human nature," that are used to rationalize groups' positions in a society (Sensoy & DiAngelo, 2017) is of paramount importance to restorative literacies. The "traditional view of meritocracy holds that most inequalities are not created by some central authority or discriminatory policy but arise out of the individual's innate or acquired skills, capabilities, education, and other resources" (Ornstein, 2007, p. 171). Education is currently the basis of achievement and economic success in our country. Yet while our students like Olivia do not start out equally, our schools continue to test, sort, and track students by gifted and talented, special education, English language learner, Title I, and intervention groups and other forms of educational stratification. Milner (2018) encourages teachers and students to recognize that oppression, discrimination, and marginalization are the central reasons why many people live in poverty, and that people of color are disproportionately represented in poverty. Therefore, we must come to see that poverty is not a "culture." Instead, it is a reaction to a lived and perceived reality. Even though Olivia came from a family with the means to hire tutors, advocates, and lawyers, her long-term educational and economic future was in jeopardy because of her segregated and uneven school experiences.

An unwillingness to listen to the impact of ethnocentrism, color- and/or identity blindness, and ideologies of meritocracy, equal opportunity, individualism, and human nature unfortunately can lead to structural and systemic ableism, deficit mindsets, and disproportionality in schools. In addition, the trouble with grit ideology, a close cousin to deficit mindsets, is that of all the combinations of barriers that most impact the educational outcomes of students experiencing poverty—which might include housing instability, food insecurity, inequitable access to high-quality schools, unjust school policies, and others—not a single one is related in any way to students' grittiness (Gorski, 2016).

Ableism

Progress toward equity is dependent first and foremost on the acknowledgment that ableism exists in schools (Hehir, 2005). Ableism is a concept that is not well understood but is one of the most societally entrenched and accepted "isms" (Wolbring, 2008). Disability is understood through the gaze of medicalization; that is, there is a biological, genetic, hormonal, neurological, or physiological condition or syndrome that is viewed as "tragic" and leads to a focus on "fixing" or "curing" the person (Goodley, 2014). Ableism rejects the variation of being, the notion of biodiversity (Wolbring, 2008).

In disabling or ableist societies, a valued citizen must be not only cognitively, socially, and emotionally able and competent, but also biologically and psychologically stable, genetically and hormonally sound, and responsible. Due to the long history of colonialism, heteronormativity, patriarchy, and class warfare, citizenship also values being White, heterosexual, male, and adult (Goodley, 2014). And to many people on Olivia's educational team, Olivia was not "normal" because of the focus on her reading and writing achievement. However, Mr. Delaney and the literacy coach together began efforts to shift this focus so that Olivia and others around her would see Olivia as a viable member of the educational community. Addressing underlying concepts of ableism may be key to addressing disciplinary issues, achievement gaps, disproportionality, and other disparities.

In restorative literacy, educators must see that within-classroom and between-classroom ability grouping based on arbitrary assessment results, previous academic achievement, or disciplinary issues has very little impact on improving student performance. But student-centered teaching in small and flexible groups based on instructional needs is very effective (Fisher et al, 2016). Mr. Delaney wanted Olivia in his classroom's small groups, book clubs, discussion circles, and even writing and blogging groups. Mr. Delaney and the literacy coach began to work with the team on returning Olivia to the general education classroom over time. Restorative literacies provide numerous opportunities for deeper conversations that are socially and emotionally situated within small and flexible groups. Furthermore, identity politics, referring to the focus on the barriers of specific groups in their struggle for equality, can be heard and addressed in restorative literacies. Landmark civil rights have been accomplished through identity politics, such as women's suffrage, the Americans With Disabilities Act, Title 9, and the federal recognition of same-sex marriages (DiAngelo, 2018). Restorative literacies, beginning with compassionate listening, provide a time and space for young people, including Olivia, to serve as changemakers for a more equitable and promising future.

DEVELOPING RELATIONSHIPS

In recognizing and keeping in check ethnocentrism, social identity, meritocracy, and deficit mindsets, educators can dig deeper into the social, emotional, and literacy needs of students. Listening to develop relationships takes a personal commitment and investment of energy. It is difficult not to like and feel closer to people who listen, who show that they value the thoughts and ideas of other people (Brownell, 2015). "Learning from student voices could prove to be especially powerful learning experiences for teachers, administrators, and policymakers who either may be removed from the realities of culturally diverse students or who do not understand the experiences of those outside of their racial and cultural groups" (Carey et al., 2018, p. 70). Not only did Olivia need to be heard, but she, her teachers, and her educational team needed to trust Olivia to express what she needed in order to grow as a striving reader and writer, and not as a student with deficits to be remediated.

Educators also can broaden their perspectives and worldviews through community immersion. Olivia and her teacher were of the same culture and language, but Mr. Delaney made an effort to know all of his students' backgrounds and to bridge these backgrounds into a sense of community in his classroom. And that meant including Olivia too. Community immersion can impact educators' understanding of their own identity and affirm the need to understand the students, their families, and the communities in which they will teach (Waddell, 2013). Developing intercultural competence, such as through classroom teaching experience, homestays or daily activity in international or domestic communities, and/or structured reflection and dialogue with local teachers and leaders, is a multifaceted and dynamic endeavor and one that is clearly a lifelong learning project for individual teacher-learners (Smolcic & Katunich, 2017). An ongoing culture of listening and reflection permeates student-centered schools (Noguera et al., 2015) and is an essential component of restorative literacies.

TRAUMA-INFORMED LISTENING

Listening to childhood trauma, a common and pervasive occurrence in schools, is crucial to restorative literacies. *Adverse childhood experiences* (ACEs) is a term used to describe all types of abuse, neglect, and other potentially traumatic experiences that occur to people across all populations under the age of 18. Almost two-thirds of surveyed adults reported at least one ACE, and more than one in five reported three or more ACEs (Centers for Disease Control, 2020). However, students who are experiencing trauma can be retraumatized in school through poorly chosen reading lessons, activities, and assignments, and tracking based on perceived academic ability (Gaffney, 2019). Schools should be a place of affirming positive identities. Students develop resilience when their struggles are acknowledged—but not erased—during the inevitable stresses of life (Gold, 2016). The impacts of childhood trauma can be mitigated by creating a healthy school ecosystem that addresses the needs of the whole child. In restorative literacies, understanding the prevalence of child trauma, the purpose of becoming a trauma-sensitive school, and the outcomes of becoming trauma-informed is crucial. It is important to understand that poor responses to reading and writing are not a maladaptive behavior. Instead, a traumatized child's brain has learned that in order to survive, it needs to remain in survival mode at all times (Plumb et al., 2016). However, educators fostering restorative literacies can observe children for indications of resilient thinking and self-efficacy beliefs in their reading and writing processes (McTigue et al., 2009). Olivia was already reading, albeit in a secret manner, and found a way to express herself through anonymous blogging. Her teacher recognized her current literacies and used them to build upon and expand them to school and other forms of literacies.

At the same time, educators and administrators also would benefit from acknowledging the impact on themselves when working with students who have been traumatized. Educators, too, need to recognize the importance of self-care and attending to self-care activities. Educators who are unable to regularly attend to their own care and who develop burnout, compassion fatigue, or vicarious trauma may be unable to adequately respond to their students (Plumb et al., 2016). Certainly, educators should take time to escape into the world of books, writing in journals, putting together a gratitude list, and other self-soothing literacies.

RESPONDING TO DIFFICULT BEHAVIOR

When pausing to differentiate difficult behaviors and trauma in schools from identity and literacies, educators should place focus on embracing identities and literacies, rather than on quickly addressing behaviors that may result in shame, isolation, further resentment, and defiance. This doesn't mean that educators should ignore difficult behaviors, but rather that they should listen to, acknowledge, and respond to the underlying feelings and needs. Having access to literacy, or even being considered literate, comes with privileges, whereas those who are perceived as illiterate, as inarticulate, or as struggling readers and writers often are relegated to second-class citizenship in both school and out-of-school spaces (Winn et al., 2019). Students who are struggling, are disfranchised, or are "disabled" in the cognitive processes of reading and writing get typecast as problems in schools and too often are met with "remediation." Instead, students like Olivia should have a voice in their needs for learning and growing.

It was not often that Olivia would have a meltdown over her reading or writing, but when she did, her meltdowns were surprising and magnified. Time-outs are a primary disciplinary technique and often thought to be an effective tool. But while time-outs usually are supposed to be for calming down, they most often fail to achieve this objective. Instead, time-outs inadvertently make students feel unheard, angrier, and more dysregulated, in addition to having to deal with feelings of shame and abandonment. Furthermore, time-outs are not linked directly and logically to a particular behavior, causing ineffective learning.

As opposed to time-outs, time-ins involve repair, such as asking a student to try again in handling a situation or to communicate differently. A gentle discussion during a time-in can acknowledge and address overwhelming feelings, such as Olivia's frustration, fear, and embarrassment. Time-ins provide students and adults a chance to pause and reflect, and to repair and build relationships. Rather than dramatically or emotionally reacting, or responding to every infraction with a one-size-fits-all strategy that ignores the context of the situation or a child's developmental stage, educators can work from principles and strategies that respect children as the individuals they are (Siegel & Bryson, 2016). Olivia responded very quickly to time-ins with Mr. Delaney and the literacy coach, and her meltdowns became both less intense and less frequent.

Meltdowns also can occur when relationships break down. For example, racial illiteracy prevents us from building and sustaining authentic relationships across racial lines. When using literacy instruction to address racial illiteracy, educators must be willing to be uncomfortable, to listen, to check their assumptions, to take risks, to speak up, and to teach all students about racism (Kaczmarczyk et al., 2019). Therefore, simply calling out students in attempts to counter hate, bigotry, or intolerance is ineffective. When students' mistakes, biases, stereotypes, or misunderstandings are pointed out, the difficult conversation is at risk of completely shutting down. Thus, educators end up not addressing or rectifying the damage, but instead publicly shaming offenders through tactics like humiliation, shunning, scapegoating, or gossiping (Ross, 2019).

Call-Ins

Ross (2019) notes that "calling-in" is the ability to speak up without tearing down. Call-ins are done with care, not with shame. Call-ins are agreements between people who listen and work together to consciously expand their perspectives in a humane and loving manner. Educators can patiently ask guiding questions to help students explore opportunities for rethinking, rephrasing, and repairing biases, stereotypes, or misunderstandings. At times, Olivia's "slowness" was pointed out publicly by her peers when, in fact, she was trying to reorient herself back to classroom activities. By recognizing Olivia's frustration and embarrassment, Mr. Delaney was able to develop call-in agreements, first through literacy instruction on a social justice topic and then throughout his entire classroom climate, for all of his students. It was not long before all of his students began to be patient and inclusive toward one another, as well as toward Olivia.

Of course, call-ins are not for everyone or for every circumstance. It's not fair, for example, to insist that people, including Olivia, who was hurt by cruel or careless language or actions, be responsible for the personal growth of those who have injured them (Ross, 2019). While calling-out techniques may be more useful for powerful people who intentionally use bigotry, fear, and lies to attack others, in most school situations where students are still learning about how to carry on difficult conversations, calling-in is more appropriate. By sharing diverse books, facilitating literature circles, and using dialogue journals, educators in restorative literacies have a perfect venue for call-ins and for encouraging a willingness to listen, check assumptions, and take risks. Coupling powerful literacy instruction with diverse books that evoke thoughts and feelings about race, abilities, and social justice can aid teachers in facilitating these much-needed conversations (Kaczmarczyk et al., 2019, p. 524).

Unfortunately, many students struggling with reading and writing, like Olivia, experience frequent call-outs, both publicly and privately, on their literacies practices and even speech and language patterns. Every time Olivia made a reading miscue, she would be stopped and corrected immediately. Every time Olivia attempted to spell a word, her misspellings would be noted and would result in a spelling drill. Every time Olivia lapsed in saying r-control vowels or did not use the correct tense of a word, she would be asked to practice the sounds or words again. And it was obvious to everyone in Olivia's class that she was being removed for "remediation" for long periods of time. It seemed to Olivia that meaning in reading and messages in writing and speaking didn't matter to the adults around her. Since Olivia felt constantly picked on, she kept hiding the books she was enjoying and kept blogging anonymously to avoid the frequent call-outs on her reading and writing. Mr. Delaney and the literacy coach encouraged everyone to refrain from correcting Olivia's errors in reading, writing, and speaking, but rather to focus on her meaning and messages. Olivia finally was able to pause, retrace her steps, and build resiliency and confidence about her reading and writing. And with that opportunity, she was able to practice reading and writing more, which in turn improved her decoding and spelling skills.

Work Avoidance

Work avoidance and mediocrity are frequent "misbehavior" in schools, and, at times, are even bragged about as students walk in halls or shuffle in and out of classrooms. Olivia was not immune to work avoidance and mediocrity. M. Johnson (2018) reminds educators that this phenomenon is common to all of us and one that educators must listen to. For example, many multitasking educators gleefully boast about how they read a book or set up their grade books while "doing" the yearly state-mandated online training on blood-borne pathogens and hazardous materials, knowing they easily will "pass" at the end of each training session. Avoidance and mediocrity become a positive state of mind because people believe they are beating a seemingly pointless system (M. Johnson, 2018). Olivia was subjected to meaningless and easy worksheets, which she avoided. But adults originally saw Olivia's avoidance as an inability to do the work, so she was provided easier worksheets, causing a vicious downward cycle of reluctance. In restorative literacy, students are encouraged to respectfully question why literature is mandated in schools. What value do we get from books? How can learning to write help in life? Why do we need to know how to argue? And as educators, we should be fully prepared to listen and respond to these questions, to make authentic connections between school and students' lives.

UPHOLDING VOICES

It is not enough to simply listen, withhold judgment, monitor multiple lenses, dig deeper, and build identities and literacies. Upholding voices, especially for disempowered students like Olivia, is crucial to restorative literacies. Students, educators, and administrators, in common with all people in human relationships, desire to be treated with dignity. Societies that force people to choose between an extreme form of collectivism and the other extreme of hyper-individualistic global capitalism are inherently unstable.

But a third way between collectivist and hyper-individualist societies is to see that we all have the need to belong, to have voice, and to exercise agency in our own affairs (Bolton, 2019).

Children and young people, like Olivia, increasingly are perceived not as passive recipients of services and policies, but as political actors in their own right. Children are more robust, articulate, and willing to be heard than many adults assume to be the case (Craig, 2003). An inclusive space can be fashioned where "student responses to texts are *always* valued and seen as a learning tool" (Winn et al., 2019, p. 46, emphasis added). In this space, restoring and re-storying can assist students with making sense of texts at hand. Recognizing the complex interrelationship among identity, behavior, and literacies is key to restorative literacies. Once educators practice listening, they can expand their views on literacies.

CHAPTER 4

Thinking About Literacies

Diego was a student of multiple languages. He was surrounded by Spanish, a variation of English noted by linguistic researchers as Black language, academic English at school, and the forms of English written in both children's books and textbooks. And Diego, an affable 3rd-grade student, didn't entirely realize that he was juggling them all. Diego, however, knew that while reading sentences, he needed to maintain his comprehension of which words were important to focus on and which to let go of in particular instances. For example, in reading the sentence, "So be a good boy and don't get into mischief" (Fleischman,1986), Diego knew that *mischief*, a word that he managed to sound out, was a key word to making sense of the sentence, but he didn't know its exact definition. On the other hand, in reading the sentence, "Prince Brat tied their powdered wigs to the backs of their oak chairs," he knew that *powdered*, another word that he sounded out, was describing a kind of wig, but he wasn't able to visualize *powdered wigs*. Diego kept reading on to see whether the words were necessarily relevant to the story or whether they would come up again in a different context. As he kept reading, Diego eventually would figure out appropriate substitutes for unknown words on his own, in both English and Spanish. He was able to determine that *mischief* was another word for *trouble*, but only after he sorted out the verbal marker *be* (as in *be a good boy*) in Black language, by first thinking that the boy was always a good boy. Finally, Diego figured out that Prince Brat was told to be a good boy because Prince Brat was always in trouble. Diego did not seem to feel anything was amiss in his literacy development. He was always trying to make meaning, comprehend, and learn new words. Since he was attempting to read books that his peers liked to read, Diego did not identify himself as a "struggling" or "low" reader.

Here was a story, but the story was not entirely Diego's story. Diego was friendly and easygoing, and took just about every challenge that came his way in stride. He was eager to learn and had many friends at school. Diego didn't mind reading, writing, or doing math. When he made an error in his schoolwork, he shrugged his shoulders or even chuckled at times, paused to learn from the error, and easily moved on. However, Ms. Evans, Diego's teacher, found Diego's reading benchmark levels and test scores abysmal. His scores consistently identified Diego as reading at a high kindergarten or low-1st-grade level, even though Diego had access to books both at school and at home, tried to read widely, and even appeared to enjoy reading. Diego consistently was building and strengthening the relationships between his linguistic backgrounds and perspectives, as well as his variable skills, proficiencies, and fluencies, and the challenging texts he was encountering.

Diego's story was actually Ms. Evans's story. At the time, Ms. Evans unfortunately was caught in the throes of teacher evaluation, in which up to 40% of her effectiveness as a teacher would be determined by student growth on trimester test scores and the scores from the annual state standardized test. Ms. Evans, an observant teacher of reading and writing, was worried not so much about Diego, but about the security of her job. After all, Diego appeared to be learning and seemed a delightfully happy child at school. Ms. Evans was distressed to see the mismatch between Diego's test scores and his capabilities. And Ms. Evans began to doubt her expertise as a teacher in the face of high-stakes testing. Thus, she requested that Diego be placed in a special education resource room to help him to improve his literacy skills. In fact, she had already encouraged Diego's parents to consider signing a referral to test him for disabilities. Diego's parents initially were not concerned about their son, but at Ms. Evans's urging that something was "wrong" with their son's scores, they began to believe that perhaps Diego was "slower" than his siblings and cousins because they never heard anything amiss from Diego's siblings' and cousins' teachers. Instead of a resource room, restorative literacies were needed right in the system that Diego and Ms. Evans found themselves in.

DEFINING LITERACIES

In addition to practicing compassionate listening, educators fostering restorative literacies can pause to reflect on the interrelationship between literacy, language, culture, identity, and power (Lazar et al., 2012). Most people usually define literacy simply as a basic and functional ability to read and write proficiently, fluently, and effectively. Perhaps the definition might include competence or knowledge about a specific field, such as workplace, academic, cultural, media, computer, or disciplinary literacy. Developing a single definition of literacy, or even a continuum or taxonomy of literacy, is complicated because literacy can be interpreted in individual, social, cultural, geographical, historical, linguistic, and political terms (Harris & Hodges, 1995). Underlying definitions of literacies in states' standardized tests or in benchmark levels for each grade, even 3rd-grade reading levels, have significant impacts on students, families, and educators, including Diego's educational trajectory and Ms. Evans's job security.

Too often, literacy in education is explained as a dichotomy between literacy and illiteracy, in that students *can* versus *can't* or *will* versus *won't* read or write. But defining concepts of literacy versus illiteracy falls in the realm of politics, not in the realm of linguistic science (Venezky et al., 1990). Operating from this dichotomy, which is rooted in standards, testing, and compliance, in turn creates a disparaging meritocracy, deficit mindsets, or grit ideology in education. Ferdman (1990) explains that "an illiterate person is someone who cannot access (or produce) texts that are seen as significant within a given culture. That same person, in another cultural context, may be classified as being quite literate. When a number of cultures co-exist within the same society, it is more likely that we will encounter variant concepts of what constitutes being literate" (p. 186). But Diego was making use of his multiple languages and literacies as best as he could, while negotiating a text involving new words like *mischief* and concepts like *powdered wigs*. Ms. Evans certainly recognized Diego's strengths and resiliency in that he *could* read, was *willing* to read, and *enjoyed* the books that his peers were reading.

There is no one form of literacy that is *right* or *legitimate*. Instead of using a single term *literacy*, a more accurate and inclusive way to describe practices that surround language and print is to say *literacies* (Barton, 2017; Lazar et al., 2012). Barton (2017) noted that an ecology of literacy is best understood as a set of practices that people use in literacy events. Conversations about literacies can be approached from social, psychological, and historical perspectives. Literacy is a social activity in which people have different literacies that they make use of in association with different domains of life. Literacy is embedded in our lives psychologically, in that we use literacy as a symbolic system to represent ourselves and in that we have awareness, attitudes, and values with respect to literacy. And literacy has a history, our personal history from early childhood onward, along with our social history in which current practices are created out of past practices. Furthermore, there are multilingual literacy practices. And not all spoken languages in the world are written down, creating another whole set of possibilities in the relationship between linguistics and literacies.

With an expanded view of *literacies*, "problems" in reading and writing can be seen in a new light and don't always point to some sort of cognitive disability such as learning disabilities, reading disorders, or dyslexia. Did Diego struggle with tests? Yes. Was Diego disabled? Most likely not. Diego was seen as mixing up Spanish, Black language, the academic English at school, and the standardized forms of English written in children's books and textbooks, when the reality was that he was always trying to make sense of his reading. Ms. Evans was concerned enough about his test scores to think that Diego would benefit from placement in a resource room. However, as the result of federal and state rules, Diego would not qualify for special education services due to an exclusionary rule for English language learners. Because Diego conversed well enough in English, he didn't qualify for English as a Second Language services either. Since Diego was already thriving in his classroom community, making friends and eager to learn, Ms. Evans also sensed that it would be detrimental to consider removing him for "remedial" purposes without first attempting to provide conversation about—and acceptance of—varieties of languages, both oral and in print, for all students in an inclusive manner. Given the systems and structures of schools, Ms. Evans was not sure how to navigate educational access for Diego.

Educators must recognize that all people confront new literacies and challenging texts at times over their lifespans. For example, a newcomer to a major city may struggle to decipher the subway schedule. Or completing complex tax forms may be difficult for many adults. Most people would prefer to read the Mayo Clinic's patient and health care information rather than an oncologist's research paper in a peer-reviewed journal. Many people, well into adulthood, are self-described bad spellers and grammarians, and use word prediction software on word processors or cell phones, or hire good editors. When schools embrace and empower an expanded view of literacies, restorative practices can promote learning about, responding to, and strengthening language, linguistics, literacies, and identities, in addition to decoding and encoding proficiency and fluency, for all students and even for educators.

EXPANDING THE LITERARY CANON

Exploring the relationship among reading, writing, literacies, languages, identity, and power requires educators to question the literary canon from elementary to high schools. The canon in literature is the body of major works that a culture considers important at a given time (Harris & Hodges, 1995). The Western canon, comprising the "classics," once was thought of as timeless and universal—a perception that is now being undermined by the combined forces of feminism, multiculturalism, and popular culture. By some accounts, the canon excluded authors from social groups that historically have been marginalized or that do not conform to the interests of the dominant culture, and therefore was condemned as an elitist, patriarchal, racist, or ethnocentric construction (Kolbas, 2018).

An essential question for teachers to ask is not only how variables outside schools affect students' access to and attainment of literacy, but also how educators choose texts and know how important the contextual understanding is to literacy (A. Johnson, 2019). Teachers generally tend to choose emotionally and politically safe books and other material for instruction and for their classroom libraries. But for many students, unfortunately, some of these books may be old, dry, or exclusionary. One reason that critical thinking is avoided at every grade level of public schooling is that it necessarily involves controversies (Noddings & Brooks, 2016). Avoiding controversies in books and discussions about books can lead to a culture of compliance, ignorance, and unquestioned respect for authority.

Instead, students should recognize a canon not just of publications, but of philosophies—and they should own their ability to contribute fresh verses to it (Kay, 2018). However, while people treasure freedom of speech, they should accept responsibility for its quality. Students can be taught how to increase their capacity for critical thinking along with maintaining a moral commitment (Noddings & Brooks, 2016). There is no better way to access critical thinking, deepen meaning, and expand our worldview than to embrace and explore the rich world of languages and literacies through expanding the literary canon. Instead of a focus on Diego's reading and writing abilities in deficit ways, his rich experiences with his languages and literacies can be brought to the forefront, benefiting both him and the students around him. Ms. Evans realized not only that Diego can learn to decode and figure out the meaning of *mischief* and *powdered wigs*, but that deep conversations surrounding these concepts can be had about the structure of power and behavior in societies.

The canonical works evident in many English classes have not changed, but the century has changed (Styslinger, 2017). We are still teaching the books and poems that our parents and even grandparents were assigned to read. Many adults don't remember reading the "classics," or may not even have read them at all. Some adults even boast about coasting through English courses through class discussions and Cliff's Notes, all the while still earning a decent grade. Monocultural approaches to literacy can cause or increase an achievement gap and disengagement with literacy (National Council of Teachers of English, 2007). The reality is that many students, even the elementary students in Diego's school, *are* reading modern young adult novels, graphic novels, and digital material outside school, but often they are reluctant to read or are not reading what is available or assigned in schools.

When educators *workshop the canon*, a process of actively and purposefully partnering classic texts with a variety of high-interest, multiple genres within a reading and writing workshop structure, they can bridge the divide between literature and literacy (Styslinger, 2017). Acknowledging how the role of history, nationalism, and patriotism plays out in textbooks and, in many cases, children's trade books is crucial for restorative literacies. In particular, history textbooks tend to exclude conflict, suspense, and grim realities, leaving out anything that might reflect badly on our national character (Loewen, 2008). A desire to shield children from the troublesome facts of our history through romanticization of our past and hero-fication of people, particularly White male leaders, alienates generations of children of color and working-class families, and girls. At the same time, it is equally important to share books that do not contain issues of oppression or reflect a victim mentality, such as one about a young Black boy working up the courage to jump off a diving board at a swimming pool (Cornwall, 2017) or about a Black girl and her hardworking mother being together on a Saturday (Mora, 2019).

Text Leveling

Students, particularly those in elementary grades and struggling secondary readers, are provided books and reading passages based solely on their "levels" in terms of text complexity. Diego was reading books that his peers were reading, even though he had low test scores. But Ms. Evans feared that if Diego was placed on a lower benchmark level because of his test scores, he would be in danger of losing ground in his educational career. Some text-leveling systems are determined by mathematical formulas using a combination of variables such as the average number of words in a sentence, the average number of syllables in words, or how frequently the words are used out of a word corpus. Other leveling systems, using alphabetic letters or grades, rate and field-test books by their text structures, illustrations and graphics, themes and content, and other book and print features. The goal is to choose books or passages for students that are not too easy or too hard but just right at their "instructional" level, regardless of the topic. But when students are provided instructional scaffolds, such as making sure Diego accesses words like *mischief* and *powdered wigs*, they have greater access to reading materials that otherwise might be determined to be at "frustration" levels—books that are far more interesting, sophisticated, and engaging. The difficulty of the text is not the real issue—instruction is (Fisher et al., 2012). In restorative literacies, the levels of the books or reading passages alone do not determine the identity of the reader in terms of their capabilities. Many other factors, such as identity, background knowledge, depth and breadth of vocabulary, interest, and motivation, can contribute to and expand literacy.

Choice and Voice

While literacy is a social practice drawing from various communities in and out of school, educators often devalue, ignore, or censor literacies that are morally suspect, raise controversial issues, or distract from more important schoolwork (National Council of Teachers of English, 2007). Inviting students to select their own books still feels like the most controversial teaching practice, but student choice is synonymous with student *engagement*. Frequent and voluminous book reading builds fluency, stamina, vocabulary, confidence, and comprehension (Atwell, 2015). Four decades of research have established that voluminous and pleasurable reading is key to literacy development, but striving readers typically lack positive experiences with reading. Since they are likely to have had many negative interactions with unappealing and difficult material, the best intervention is a good book (Harvey & Ward, 2017). Since Ms. Evans did not have much control over the nature of standardized testing and benchmarks, she decided to enrich her literacies program more deeply and widely, not only for Diego but for all of her students.

Restorative literacies necessitate that educators see that preserving space and time for choice and voice leads to volume. Volume in turn leads to building surface skills, such as decoding proficiency and fluency, and deeper meaning, including vocabulary and comprehension. And good books can be used as gateways to new books, even connecting to works that are assigned by teachers or schools. Extending the reach for literature beyond the classics (or leveled books) does not weaken the quality of literature instruction. Doing so can amplify and enrich students' literary experiences, while both affirming students' own lives and engaging them in worlds very different from their own (Zapata et al., 2018). In restorative literacies, a focus on increasing the volume of self-chosen, independent, and silent reading, along with conversations about literacies, is more likely to foster surface skills such as fluency, vocabulary, and comprehension as well.

Unfamiliar Genres and Academic Literacy

Diego enjoyed writing, particularly texting, too. Even though cell phones were not allowed in his 3rd-grade classroom, Diego frequently reported that he loved to text with various members of his family. Reading and writing develop in interrelated and reciprocated ways. "Young writers find out what kinds of writers they are by experiment. If they choose from the outset to practice exclusively a form of writing because it is praised in the classroom or otherwise carries appealing prestige, they are vastly increasing the risk inherent in taking up writing in the first place. It is so easy to misjudge yourself and get stuck in the wrong genre" (McPhee, 2017, p. 79). Avoiding this risk early on, however, means dabbling widely, in both reading and writing, in every genre, even unfamiliar ones in unfamiliar variations of languages and linguistics. Ms. Evans not only delved into expansive reading practices but also broadened experiences in writing. Genre studies offer students a way to explore the multifaceted nature of written texts and the multiple processes that writers might use for various genres. Through broad and deep exploration of written texts, students can learn that while a eulogy is distinctive from a memoir or an essay, all can share life experiences, and that while satires and editorials have different features, both can be used as persuasive pieces (Fleischer & Andrew-Vaughan, 2009).

Contrary to the myth that Google and Facebook are frying our brains, even among a generation of tweeters and texters, students are writing a lot, both in class and out; the length of their writing has increased nearly threefold in 25 years. "Complaints are made about children's poor literacy, and then, when a technology arrives that provides fresh and motivating opportunities to read and write, such as email, chat, blogging, and texting, complaints are made about that" (Crystal, 2008, p. 157). Users of technology are increasingly aware of their audiences and know to write differently for a teacher or professor than for a casual friend. And they want their writing to account for something and increasingly see writing as a collaborative, social, and participatory activity rather than a solitary one (Lunsford, 2013). Children could not be good at texting if they had not already developed considerable literacy awareness. Before they can write abbreviated forms effectively and play with them, they need to have a sense of how the sounds of their language relate to the letters and alternative spelling. Furthermore, there is increasing evidence that texting helps, rather than hinders, literacy (Crystal, 2008).

On the flip side, students are likely *reading* more too. Students, including Diego, are saturated with media, text messaging, social networking, and digital video filmmaking. It is not necessary to either praise or condemn this new media age, but we should advocate for a *critical media education*, which, in turn, can lead to academic literacy development, academic achievement, and civic engagement. Critical media fosters an awareness of the positive and negative role that media plays. Critical media, which applies in both literature and social studies courses, can provide space for rigorous, relevant, participatory, authentic, and engaging opportunities to enact social change (Morrell et al., 2013).

Just as educators must become aware of the multiple languages and literacies of their students like Diego, and of a wider range of genres than is normally taught in schools, students need to be made aware of disciplinary literacies in an explicit and authentic manner. Reading, writing, and thinking like a historian are vastly different than reading, writing, and thinking like a scientist. Academic literacy is the ability to communicate, through reading, writing, and presenting, competently in an academic discourse community. Too often, subject-area teachers feel responsible for teaching only the content of the subject, not the literacies associated with the field. Problems with academic literacy traditionally have been attributed to students being preconceived of as disadvantaged or deficient, but the way in which language is used in academic discourse is rarely made explicit to students (Wingate, 2015). Thus, only a select few students, who are already familiar with academic and/or disciplinary literacy through their home or school lives, are successful. As a result of listening to Diego's reading capabilities in a strength-based manner, Ms. Evans began to see the far-reaching depths of literacies, that is, the cultural, linguistic, economic, political, and dis/ableist views along with the cognitive and metacognitive processes of reading proficiency, fluency, and comprehension, as well as writing encoding and effectiveness.

MINDING GAPS BETWEEN
READING PROCESSES AND READING INSTRUCTION

For purposes of reading intervention, it is not enough to simply provide students with intriguing books. Teachers also must provide space and time for instruction, and practice on how to choose material and actually read—decode—the text. But when considering reading instruction, educators can't think about aspects of reading in isolation (Willingham, 2017). An expansion of the cognitive and metacognitive processes in reading and writing requires thinking beyond just phonics, sight words, vocabulary, fluency, and comprehension as separate skills being taught in a vacuum. Too often, there is a significant gap between how a proficient reader reads and how a student labeled as "disabled" or "struggling" is *instructed* in how to read. Underlying deficit definitions of learning disabilities, dyslexia, or otherwise "struggling readers" can also maintain insidious gaps between theories of language, cognition, reading processes, educational assessments, and/or standardized testing. The present-day controversies over reading instruction methods and assessments require understanding that philosophical and psychological underpinnings have contributed to views of how children become readers, ranging from nature (biology) versus nurture (experience), models of reading acquisition, and various proposals of developmental stages of reading (Farrall, 2012).

Diego's reading ability was evaluated on a thrice-yearly benchmark assessment that included checks for oral reading accuracy and comprehension questions. Since his rate of accuracy in reading a passage was measured at 86%, below the criterion of 95%, Diego was assessed at lower-level benchmarks until he achieved the acceptable rate of reading accuracy. Once he was found to be able to read with at least 95% accuracy, he was asked comprehension questions. Because Diego, as a 3rd-grader, was reading an early-1st-grade-level text, the comprehension questions were quite simple for him to answer correctly. Finding Diego to be at a 1st-grade level in reading alarmed Ms. Evans, who didn't think that his scores were reflective of his reading ability.

On the state standardized test, Diego managed to read most of the passages online, but he struggled with choosing single words in a multiple-choice format in order to answer comprehension questions. Diego resorted to guessing, and when he completed the test, he found a book to read while contentedly waiting for his peers to finish. Needless to say, Diego's reading score was rated "not proficient." Diego's referral process required more testing to determine whether he would be eligible for special education services. Again, Diego was asked to read passages aloud, and again he skipped words that he wasn't sure of and, in an attempt to make sense of the passages, in several cases returned to the words he had skipped to make corrections or substitutions. However, in this particular test, all omissions, substitutions, repeats, and self-corrections were scored as errors, placing Diego in the 5th percentile. Diego answered some of the comprehension questions easily, but since the passages were taken away from him immediately after he read them out loud to the examiner, he was not able to refer to them. He was not able to point to and reread some of the words he suspected were key words in answering some of the vocabulary questions.

As Ms. Evans realized, without someone observing Diego taking these assessments and tests and having conversations with him about his negotiations of the passages, the scores would not reveal that Diego was using the very strategies that proficient and fluent readers use when confronting challenging material. "Difficulties" in reading and writing are most often a result of devastating *opportunity gaps* that students have faced early in their elementary years because of subtle political, systemic, and discriminatory barriers in schools, particularly when assessments and test scores are given considerable weight in making educational decisions for students. These gaps tend to stay with students throughout their entire educational career, at times leading to unwarranted placement in special education, disciplinary issues, or even dropping out altogether. By shifting from reliance on test scores to careful observation, from deficit mindsets to strength-based mindsets, and from a focus on an achievement gap (outcome) to an opportunity gap (cause), educators can begin to see that gaps in opportunities are a precursor to gaps in achievement (Milner, 2010; Wolter, 2015). We must expand not only the canon in our schools, but also our notion of what is involved in being a strategic reader.

A problematic area in the discussion about opportunity gaps in literacy instruction is a systemic fixation on seeking a reading "program" or a different tier in the multitiered system of support, usually of a prescriptive, commercial, or online nature, that would meet the needs of students who fail to maintain an on-schedule pace of reading acquisition. Poor readers, both historically and currently, experience a curriculum quite different from that of their better-reading peers. "Low-achieving readers are more likely to be asked to read aloud than silently, to have their attention focused on word recognition rather than comprehension, to spend more time alone on low-level worksheets than on reading authentic texts, and to experience more fragmentation in their instructional activities" (Walmsley & Allington, 2007, p. 29). Instead, teachers need the space to expand their expertise in reading processes and instruction. From what Ms. Evans knew about Diego's actual ability to tackle challenging material, the kinds of instructional methods typically reserved for low-achieving readers would not meet Diego's needs for enriching literacy development.

In restorative literacies, a focus on varied instructional strategies that follow readers and their needs, rather than a rigid series of steps, can be powerfully effective (M. Howard, 2009). This involves being a teacher who observes and interacts with individual students, like Diego, as they are reading, and attends not only to the story and its meaning, but also to how the student is working on print to get those understandings. In essence, the teacher must be reflective and responsive to how the students negotiate the text (Clay, 1993). When the focus is solely on assessments and test scores, educators too often miss the cognitive processes of reading and writing in conversations with students. How do people choose books to read? What is the purpose for reading a text? What do people do when they are stuck on unknown words? What do people do if they don't understand the meaning of a particular word? There is no one *right* way to read or one *right* way to learn to read. Conversations, reflection, and feedback about both sociocultural and cognitive processes in multiple literacies are crucial to restorative literacies.

Building Metacognitive Awareness

Readers who are thought to be "disabled" or "struggling" tend to be exposed extensively to reading instruction programs or methods that teach "reading" in a fragmented and isolated manner, particularly phonics. While the ability to decode letter–sound relationships is crucial, it is by far not the only strategy for reading. Studies of proficient readers have shown the complexity of the reading process, but when we consider reading education, we shouldn't think about aspects of reading in isolation. For example, long practice sessions studying letter–sound relationships may improve decoding, but also may prompt a decline in reading motivation (Willingham, 2017). Unfortunately, in schools we fill struggling readers' days with tasks that require little reading. Such tasks involve tedious worksheets, bland decodable texts, slow and interrupted round-robin reading, or so-called educational computer programs. If we want to foster reading development, then we must design instruction and support that provide the opportunities for struggling readers to actually read (Allington, 2013).

When students are taught fragmented and isolated reading skills in a vacuum—decoding, fluency, vocabulary, or literal versus inferential comprehension—we risk their becoming disenfranchised word-by-word readers and seeing reading as a chore rather than a source of personal pleasure and knowledge. Even though Diego's test scores were "abysmally low," Ms. Evans recognized Diego's strengths in becoming a capable metacognitive reader. Metacognitive readers have the awareness and knowledge of their mental processes so that they can monitor, regulate, and self-mediate their reading and comprehension (Harris & Hodges, 1995). Metacognitive readers can read silently and deeply in a nonlinear manner, thoughtfully returning to miscued words and misread phrases to think about their meaning. They read ahead and reread. They think about the text and carry an inner voice to negotiate the information being conveyed. Metacognitive readers know that decoding helps comprehension but also that background knowledge and comprehension help decoding at the same time (Wolter, 2017). And they make sure they take away something, pleasure or knowledge or both, from their reading.

Building Metalinguistic Awareness

Not only can students become metacognitively aware of their reading processes, but they also can develop metalinguistic awareness. Diego was on his way to developing an awareness of his transfers and usage of Spanish, Black language, academic English, and standardized forms of English. And he benefited from Ms. Evans's acknowledgment and instruction when he tried to figure out multiple words and phrases in an authentic context. Many people in our global society use spoken languages or variations of languages containing phonemic, grammatical, or lexical features that are not historically or currently written down (Crystal, 2010). Unfortunately, there is a common misconception, akin to the literacy/illiteracy dichotomy, that there is good English and, following from that, bad English (Lippi-Green, 2012). The myth that nonstandard dialects of English are grammatically deficient is widespread. In fact, language is a complex, specialized, and instinctive skill, which develops spontaneously, without conscious effort or formal instruction (Pinker, 2003). Children, including Diego, by nature are biologically capable of absorbing the language around them and can, on their own, come up with increasingly complex phrasing, but that doesn't mean it is unnecessary to nurture language simply because individuals are born with a biological instinct for language.

To acquire language, both our brain's physical equipment and our society are indispensable (Coulmas, 2013). Linguistic research has shown that language variation, such as southern English and African American English, is a normal process and that differences in regions, among communities, and across time are not the same as language deficits, errors, mistakes, or confusions (Hudley & Mallinson, 2015). However, listeners predictably will make assumptions about a speaker on the basis of language markers that signal alliance with certain social groups, primarily those having to do with race, ethnicity, and economic factors (Lippi-Green, 2012). Educators should be aware of the powerful social stereotyping in which people judge speakers' intelligence, character, and personal worth on the basis of their language (Stubbs, 2002). Since people can understand language better than they can express themselves, recognizing that language that gets the job done, although it is not perfect, is good enough (Everett, 2017) is also crucial to restorative literacies. Ms. Evans, in her process of expanding and delving into literacies, learned to pay more attention to the diverse features of languages and linguistics.

Metalinguistic readers have a conscious awareness of language as an object in itself (Harris & Hodges, 1995). Metalinguistic readers who are bilingual or speak a variation of English know that the phonemes and syntax of their spoken language do not always transfer to or match exactly the language presented in text (Wolter, 2017). Diego was on the cusp of recognizing himself as a metalinguistic speaker and reader. But even monolingual speakers of English know that written text most often is not simply transcribed speech. Text is only a reflection of speech in terms of its structure; features of punctuation, capitalization, special organization, color, and other graphic effects; grammatical and lexical differences; formality; and permanence (Crystal, 2010). This is why proficient and fluent readers who read aloud adjust some words and phrases as they speak. But the practice of expecting students to read texts aloud, often with the expectation of high accuracy and fluency, is dominant in remedial and special education classrooms, and even among English language learners like Diego, who *was* trying to make sense of what he was reading by reading ahead and checking himself for the meaning of key words. Teachers interrupt poor readers more quickly and are more likely to pronounce words for them, which does not contribute to fluency or even the development of problem-solving and self-regulating strategies necessary in order to become good independent readers (Allington & McGill-Franzen, 2010). In restorative literacies, a focus on increasing the volume of self-chosen, independent, and silent reading, along with metacognitive and metalinguistic *conversations* about literacies, is more likely to foster surface skills such as fluency, vocabulary, and comprehension.

Code-Switching and Translanguaging

Our increasingly global and complex world exposes us to a rich diversity of languages and language variations of English, along with social media and texting languages, emoticons, abbreviations, acronyms, and so on. When educators begin to expand their understanding about languages, a distinction among learning English, code-switching, and translanguaging will become apparent. Code-switching is the use, with varying degrees of skill, by multilingual people of separate linguistic systems or named national languages. Translanguaging is defined by Otheguy et al. (2015) as "the deployment of a speaker's full linguistic repertoire without regard for watchful adherence to the socially and politically defined boundaries of named (and usually national and state) languages" (p. 283). In other words, we all share thousands of linguistic features with people with whom we interact a lot, whether we are multilingual or monolingual. Therefore, an outsider's perspective may see a "mixing" of phonemes, morphemes, and words, but from an insider's perspective, these linguistic features inherently belong to the speakers. A distinction in terms of socially defined categories can be made between a person who is translanguaging versus a person who is code-switching (Otheguy et al., 2015). While there is certainly nothing wrong with code-switching, in restorative literacies translanguaging should be embraced as well. Ms. Evans was wondering at first whether Diego was mixing up his languages as if he might have had some sort of cognitive processing deficit, but she realized it was entirely possible that Diego was translanguaging while attempting to read his book about a boy making mischief.

In addition to acknowledging linguistic features of different languages, educators can recognize many literacies. Literacy practices vary across cultures, and students come to school with a variety of literacy and language experiences that may not match those that are practiced or valued in school. Therefore, a more accurate and inclusive way of describing practices that surround language and print is to use the term *literacies* (Lazar et al., 2012). Neither Diego nor other students are carrying completely blank slates, in that they are so-called "illiterate," but they have had both negative and positive experiences with languages and literacies, just like the rest of us.

In restorative literacies, there is acceptance of how students negotiate all of their linguistic features and literacies in a positive manner. Diego's teacher was paying attention to all of the linguistic features appearing in her classroom. By expanding her mindset about translanguaging and code-switching in a nonjudgmental manner, she was better able to embrace Diego's, and *all* of her students', exploration of all kinds of languages, linguistics, and literacies.

Vocabulary for a Lifespan

Vocabulary is certainly a component of literacy, but educators cannot expand an understanding about vocabulary without also considering sentence meaning and social context. For example, a cup might be a *mug*, a *fruit cup*, or an *egg cup*, or words might be used idiomatically, such as *it's raining cats and dogs*. Young children expand their vocabulary quite explosively from their first identifiable word. From the time children reach 2 years old, there is such a dramatic increase in the size and diversity of their lexicon that it has not yet proved possible to make accurate calculations of the number of words they know. While phonological features (accents) and grammar are largely developed by the teen years, semantic development continues through the school years and throughout adult life (Crystal, 2010). Diego was learning new words like *mischief* and *powdered wigs*, and was capable of continually learning over his lifetime.

All people, monolingual, multilingual, and new language learners, build upon their language acquisition through learning new words over a lifespan. However, there is an assumption that a high level of reading failure among children living in poverty is linked to the claim that poor children lack the rich and varied vocabulary needed to succeed in school (Dudley-Marling & Lucas, 2009). This assumption was influenced by an oft-cited research study estimating a 30-million word gap between children in professional families and children in welfare families (Hart & Risley, 2003). However, due to theoretical and methodological weaknesses in this study, as well as its negative educational and social implications, the idea of "word gaps" must be rejected. Instead, educators should look at this issue through a language socialization lens, in that students from low economic backgrounds struggle at school not because they are linguistically or cognitively inferior to other groups, but because they enter school operating from different cultural and linguistic schemas (E. J. Johnson, 2015). Diego did not have a word gap or the inability to learn new words, but he simply did not have the knowledge of *mischief* and *powdered wigs* at the moment of Ms. Evans's observation.

Students deemed "impoverished" in language and literacies may find themselves at risk for *linguistic overprotection*. Linguistic overprotection, a term used primarily in deaf studies, occurs when people intentionally reduce, or water down, the linguistic complexity of their communication, such as using the word *sick* instead of *infectious disease*. Even with the best of intentions, White liberals (some of whom are educators) unwittingly may draw on negative stereotypes in a "likely well-meaning, 'folksy,' but ultimately patronizing, attempt to connect" with racial minorities, resulting in competence downshift in the use of their language (Dupree & Fiske, 2019, p. 580).

Linguistic overprotection and competence downshifts do not allow the opportunity for students to learn and use more sophisticated words having different connotations. There is little to be gained by pathologizing the language and culture of children living in poverty; all children, including Diego, come to school with extraordinary linguistic, cultural, and intellectual resources, just not the *same* resources (Dudley-Marling & Lucas, 2009). In restorative literacies, through many conversations about language, literacies, and reading and writing processes, educators can draw on the strengths and resources of students *and* provide access to the language practices valued in school.

LITERACIES IN CONTEXT

In restorative literacies, expanded conversations about the process of reading *in context* are paramount. It is not possible for teachers to know all the possible combinations of languages, variations of languages, and literacies that students bring to school. In fact, Ms. Evans and other teachers may feel overwhelmed and out of control when confronting unfamiliar languages, variations of language, and literacies, especially when they are trying to teach to the curricular standards. Imagine students, like Diego, confronting unfamiliar languages and literacies as they come to school. They, too, are overwhelmed and out of control, resulting in guarded or unwanted behaviors. But educators and schools are the ones with the power. And with that systemic and structural power, schools inherently determine who will succeed and who will not.

Surface skills, such as decoding, fluency, vocabulary, and comprehension, can be taught in the context of authentic and purposeful literacies through the expansion of the literary canon in schools, providing space and time for reading and writing, developing metacognition and metalinguistic awareness, allowing translanguaging, and building vocabulary for a lifespan. "Problems" in literacies do not always point to cognitive defects but can lead to meaningful negotiation of challenging material. Educational gaps are lessened when we recognize the need for restoring connections and repairing misconnections between literacies, languages, identity, and power. Once educators have expanded the definitions of languages, linguistics, and literacies, they can begin to move toward restoring relationships.

CHAPTER 5

Restoring Relationships

Ms. Morgan was in a quandary. She was only in her 1st year as principal of a K–8 school after decades of teaching 2nd and 3rd grades, but Ms. Morgan felt up to the challenge. She anticipated that if the superintendent called a snow day, she would hear from parents who thought it was prudent to close school but at the same time she would hear from parents who declared that school didn't need to be closed. She expected that she would hear from parents who felt that children should have longer recesses and from other parents who felt that children should stay indoors for more instruction. She knew she would have to balance the needs of her school and the budget. She knew she would have to work with the needs of the families in her school, especially in light of poverty, immigration, or childhood stress and trauma, and would have to provide leadership and counsel in times of crises, while simultaneously supporting the needs of her staff. And she knew she would hear from parents questioning the appropriateness of certain books in the classroom or school libraries. No matter, Ms. Morgan was excited to lead an invigorating team of educators and a diverse population of students.

But Ms. Morgan was surprised at the intensity of pressure from just a few parents surrounding the reading and writing achievement tests, benchmarks, and report cards of their children. One parent took her angry complaint that the teachers were not appropriately teaching the basics, specifically phonics, to the superintendent and the head of the state department of education. The same parent also made frequent attacks against the school on social media sites. Other parents were concerned about the "drill and kill" method of teaching reading, decrying that their children wouldn't want to come to school. A renewed national debate, namely, the "reading wars" about the "best way" to teach reading and prevent dyslexia, embroiled the conversations among parents, community members, and teachers in Ms. Morgan's school community. As a result, teacher morale was beginning to falter.

Ms. Morgan knew that teachers, in a highly demanding profession, have their individual strengths and weaknesses. She knew that teachers, some with just a few years under their belt and others with decades of teaching experience, have wide-ranging competencies in their ability to foster literacy development, including phonics instruction. And she knew that all children, having a diversity of cultural, linguistic, economic, political, and dis/ableist backgrounds, learn and grow at different rates. Ms. Morgan wanted to champion her teachers and the school in a positive light and restore relationships between her school and community.

Although many stories in education belong to our students and their educators, people mustn't forget that our school administrators have stories too. Ms. Morgan wanted to close the achievement gap and reduce disproportionality in her school among *all* of her students, not just the select few who had particularly vocal parents. Ms. Morgan wasn't sure how to approach a volatile situation that arose when of one of her teachers and she herself were being publicly disparaged and at the same time she needed to figure out how to support the teacher, who was still honing her teaching craft. Should she place herself solely in a supervisory role and require the teacher to follow the district's reading curriculum, and set an expectation for scheduled evidence of growth in the children of outspoken parents? Or should she take the role of a literacy coach and provide confidential job-embedded professional learning and reflection? Or should she simply purchase the phonics program that the parents insisted on and see to it that teachers implemented the program with fidelity?

Ms. Morgan worried that the line between supervision and coaching would get blurry. A supervisory role, especially in light of the public confrontations, would get in the way of an emotionally safe place where the teacher could challenge herself, make mistakes, and grow professionally. And Ms. Morgan worried that the boundary between giving in to the complaints from parents and backing her teachers would be a fine line to walk. Fretting over the achievement gap, Ms. Morgan was relieved to find out that highly qualified literacy coaches were being hired in each of her district's school buildings. Literacy coaches are not the sole answer to satisfying parental anger and closing achievement gaps, but this was an opportunity for restorative literacies for the entire school community.

TESTING AND VULNERABILITY

Tests do not accurately reflect a child's intelligence and competence. Few people will accept that any test score can define a child, but parents and educators have fallen into the trap of believing that academic accomplishment is the sole basis for achieving a well-lived life (J. Fox, 2008). Myriads of tests put students at the mercy of school systems when test results are used to determine student abilities and sort and track groups of students according to their abilities, and even carry consequences in the form of rewards or reprimands, such as grades, retention, or promotion.

Restorative literacies focus on the authenticity of people, on who people, and their literacies, are in the moment and over a lifespan. Ms. Morgan was well aware of vulnerabilities all around her, among her students, their parents, and her teachers. "When we spend our lives waiting until we're perfect or bulletproof before we walk into the arena, we ultimately sacrifice relationships and opportunities that may not be recoverable, we squander our precious time, and we turn our backs on our gifts" (Brown, 2015, p. 2). Too often, schools test, teach, or even wait for students to arrive at some sort of academic place without allowing them to develop the willingness, engagement, and courage to take ownership of their vulnerability. Vulnerability is not a weakness, but a brave dare to show up and be seen (Brown, 2015).

FOSTERING LOVE OF LITERACIES

An essential component of restorative practice is to restore relationships—not only relationships between students and educators, but also students' relationships with books or other texts and their authors. Fred Rogers, of *Mister Rogers' Neighborhood*, remembered his key advisor and collaborator on his show saying to an artist visiting her early childhood classes, "I don't want you to teach sculpting. All I want you to do is love clay in front of the children" (King, 2018). The children caught the artist's enthusiasm for sculpting, and that was what mattered. Of course, there is much more to teaching reading and writing than simply inviting 4- or 5-year-old children to play with books. But there is a profound truth to Mr. Rogers's advisor's request to show love. In our current climate of standards and testing in schools, people have forgotten this love for curiosity—for other people and for literacies.

Love was an area of concern for Ms. Morgan as she confronted significant racial gaps in her school, especially as they related to Black male students. School is often a place where many Black students feel as though they are despised, feared, and deemed to be of little human value. Furthermore, through a dynamic interplay of low expectations, anxieties around criminality, and racialized educational tracking, Black boys are pushed out of schools and into prisons at alarming rates (Givens & Suad Nasir, 2019). Additionally, people with disabilities generally are not thought of as having a political, social, spiritual, or even sexual identity. People with disabilities need awareness and cooperation from other people who do not experience challenges in moving from isolation to community, ignorance to knowledge, exclusion to access, and shame to pride (Garland-Thomson, 2016. In other words, all humans need connection and love to live their lives fully and to embrace the lives of other people around them.

Educators must remember that it's not just students who need restorative care in love of literacies, but that teachers also must value and engage in the act of reading. In order to influence their students' reading behaviors and attitudes in positive ways, teachers must read too, not only professional materials but also texts that they find personally interesting and compelling. Teachers who read more than 30 minutes a day for pleasure used a greater number of instructional best practices than teachers who read less than 10 minutes a day or did not read at all (McKool & Gespass, 2009). Unfortunately, teachers seldom are seen reading (Trelease, 2006). Many teachers, preoccupied with literacy skill acquisition, are successful in communicating that reading is important, but few teachers are successful in communicating that reading is enjoyable. Teachers who are avid readers talk about books in the context of pleasure, are seen to read independently at school, and read aloud to their classes with expression and emotional connection. Models of keen recreational book reading may be particularly important for children who lack such a model at home or in their friendship groups (Merga, 2016). Ms. Morgan, her literacy coach, and her librarian began the process of promoting a love for books by developing book exchanges, intergenerational book clubs, and a bulletin board that encouraged people of all ages to write a short blurb about the books they were reading at the time.

LITERACIES IN COMMUNITIES AND SCHOOLS

Since most people live and work within small social circles or peruse narrow algorithm-controlled social media, expanding literacies with intention and purpose is crucial to deepening our understanding of our global humanity. Even the social circle of parents that challenged Ms. Morgan about the reading instruction at her school was a small group. These parents read items on the Internet about dyslexia and reading instruction that were not always accurate or reflective of current research. At the same time, they were part of the professional community, working as physicians, lawyers, and corporate leaders, with little time for reading and researching in a deeper sense. And they were not cognizant of the varying literacy instruction needs of the diverse population in their schools, or of the expanded social concepts of what it means to be literate. Using their power of privilege and voice, they insisted that the teachers in Ms. Morgan's school must be trained in the explicit teaching of phonics to help their own and other children learn to read on grade level. Ms. Morgan felt the need to restore relationships with the proponents of phonics instruction and at the same time not allow them to pursue a dogma that would not benefit the entire student population.

However, another small subset of parents at Ms. Morgan's school held a weekly book club while their children were attending school. They had read on news media that reading fiction was found to prompt improvement in empathy, a necessary trait in our current climate of political polarization. Character-based stories encourage a sense of shared humanity and invite us to engage in many circumstances and to experience many emotions in relation to many kinds of people (Oatley, 2016). The possibility that reading fiction may enhance social cognitive skills in the general population or in individuals with social cognitive deficits makes reading fiction worthwhile (Dodell-Feder & Tamir, 2018). After hearing through the parent grapevine about the rise of dyslexia diagnoses and push for phonics instruction, the book club was responsive to Ms. Morgan's dilemma, rather than insistent that phonics be taught. Having time on their hands, the book club members asked whether they could volunteer as readers, tutors, and library builders. This became an opportunity for relationships to be restored, not only between school and home, but also between reading and writing instruction at school and the literacies in the community.

ACCESS, LIBRARY CULTURE, AND DIVERSITY

When there are no or few books, book reading becomes an occasion and not a routine. This has enormous consequences for children's reading development and school success. Ms. Morgan and her literacy team saw that they needed to restore relationships among people, books, and authors. But they were startled to find that even among their school was situated in a major research university town with a history of high academic achievement and ample social resources, almost a quarter of their students qualified for reduced-price meals and snacks at the school. Digging deeper, they discovered that many of these students reported that they had few or no books at home to read for fun. Unfortunately, there are stark disparities in access to print among income-segregated areas. *Book deserts*, like the healthy food desert construct, have significant consequences for the well-being of families (Neuman & Moland, 2019).

Public libraries often are seen as an equalizer in that every child, regardless of whether they came from poor neighborhoods, would have equal access to high-quality books and to computer technology. But transformative urban libraries, after substantial renovations and increased technology, did not succeed in producing equal outcomes in terms of children's qualitative use of books and technology. Children in low-income areas entered libraries alone or with a peer, sometimes with a sibling, but rarely with an adult, and had very little direction and engagement with library resources. Rather than promoting reading, items associated with technology, such as playing with keyboards, doing gaming activities without text, or otherwise engaging in short bursts of low-level activities, appeared to displace reading for low-income-neighborhood children. Libraries need to level the playing field with equal resources and then tip the balance by providing additional resources and access in low-income areas, such as ensuring highly trained librarians, creating knowledge-centered environments for children, offering mentorship, and providing culturally relevant pedagogy and learning opportunities (Neuman & Celano, 2006).

It was easy for some of Ms. Morgan's teachers to encourage the use of their town library by inviting the librarians to read aloud to their classes, setting up opportunities for students to obtain a library card, and even taking field trips to the library. While encouraging students and their parents to access their libraries is noble, much more reflection and collaboration are needed to bridge the divide between people who are disenfranchised and people who are entirely comfortable with and able to use library services. Libraries are seen as places for books, and librarians as their caretakers, but the hard truth, especially for people who see the library as one of society's truly accessible and democratic institutions, is that the subtle, insidious, and ingrained library culture is a formidable barrier for socially excluded people. Alienation results from embarrassment at not understanding how the library works; exclusionary practices relating to the inability to obtain library cards or pay fines, replacement costs, and processing fees; a feeling that the library is like school; and the belief system that libraries are only for smart or educated people (DeFaveri, 2005).

Fortunately, the library near Ms. Morgan's school had already taken steps toward breaking down barriers by training their staff on antiracism, waiving fees, modernizing the rooms, offering a makerspace, and lending everyday tools, works of art, puzzles, and games. While it may seem that free, open, and casual libraries or book exchanges that are unattached to a formal institution, such as the Little Free Libraries or thriving thrift shops, would adequately serve children and families in marginalized areas, they too tend to be installed in affluent areas; contain books that mostly depict White, affluent characters; and don't seem to be used very often (Snow, 2015). Therefore, while Ms. Morgan and her literacy team continued to encourage the use of library services, place books on a table for free exchange, and stock the Little Free Library outside the school, they took a harder look at issues of access.

Not only is access to books, technology, and other knowledge-based material an issue for some marginalized populations, but the lack of diverse characters, experiences, viewpoints, and authors is problematic for *all* populations. Therefore, the National Council of Teachers of English (2015) advocates for increased publication of culturally diverse literature that reflects human, cultural, linguistic, and family diversity. However, "it is not that individuals within the children's book industry *consciously intend* to act in ways that sustain institutional racism. It's rather that the system tends to prevent its participants from attaining a full awareness of their role in perpetuating its values" (Nel, 2017, p. 7, emphasis in original). For example, publishers advance color-blind racism via the language of business, such as by alleging that there is not much of a market for diverse stories.

Educators, administrators, librarians, and literacy coaches fostering restorative practices should prioritize seeking and reading titles about diverse characters as well as those written by diverse authors. Therefore, Ms. Morgan encouraged her literacy coach, the school librarian, and several willing parents to take a close look at the representation of race, languages, and disabilities in the books housed in their classrooms, library, book exchange table, and the Little Free Library. She also called upon enthusiastic staff members and community volunteers to apply for grants and seek donations, peruse online databases, purchase and distribute sets of diverse books in classrooms, and invite people to either present book blurbs or read aloud some of the books.

Ms. Morgan also turned to the parent book club to continue restoring relationships between the school and community. The book club members had just read *The Immortal Life of Henrietta Lacks* (Skloot, 2017), a bestseller about a poor Black tobacco farmer whose cells, known by scientists as HeLa, were instrumental toward developing the polio vaccine, cloning, gene mapping, and other medical advancements. While Henrietta Lacks's cells were profitable to research firms, her descendants remained unable to afford health insurance, creating questions about ethics and race. Two book club members gave a short presentation to a small group of 8th-graders about the book and what the members learned from it. The students didn't need to have read the book, but were still full of questions and concerns. One Black student, whose grandparents moved north during the Great Migration, went so far as to explain that his parents signed up for ancestry testing from 23andMe. His grandparents were vocally against his parents "donating" their genes based on their fear of unethical medical studies on Black people, such as the Tuskegee Syphilis Study. But he also overheard his father talking about an article or a book about DNA and social reparations for slavery and Jim Crow laws. He remarked that he couldn't avoid hearing the loud arguments in his home for or against genetic testing services. The controversy in his home manifested anew right in his classroom with his peers and the book club members. The book club members brought five copies of the book for the classroom library, but the books quickly and enthusiastically were taken before they were even shelved. The discussion not only enticed some students to read the book; it also widened the worldview of the book club members, both of whom were White and didn't think of the far-reaching and current implications, even among the 8th-graders in their school, of genetic studies, ancestry, and social reparations.

Ms. Morgan and her literacy team knew that restoring readers starts with students selecting their own books to read. This freedom was not a future, perhaps-by-spring goal for them, but a first accomplishment as a class (Miller, 2010). While school libraries are avenues for providing access to texts, classroom libraries may be even more important because they can provide immediate and more frequent access to books (Harmon et al., 2019). Educators should give thoughtful and deliberate consideration to the use of classroom library space, complete with comfortable seating, book covers that are displayed to entice readers rather than shelved by their spines, a good organizational system for access, and plenty of time to read. "The more books there are, especially books created by BIPOC authors and illustrators, the more opportunities librarians, teachers, parents, and other adults have of finding outstanding books for young readers and listeners that reflect dimensions of their lives, and give a broader understanding of who we are as a nation" (Cooperative Children's Book Center, 2020). Ms. Morgan, the literacy coach, and the librarian had no trouble garnering enthusiasm for flooding their classrooms and schools with literacies. Ms. Morgan realized she needed only to provide permission for the *love* of reading to happen rather than focusing on disparities in educational data and acquisition of skills.

MOTIVATION AND ENGAGEMENT

While classroom libraries certainly can benefit students, the benefits come to fruition only if children interact meaningfully with the books. Ms. Morgan knew this. She knew that students need instruction in order to learn to read and read well. Even if it seems that many students learn to read "naturally," some even before they arrive in kindergarten, reading is not an instinctive process like listening and speaking (Pinker, 2003). Access must move beyond availability to include opportunities for circulating and reading the texts. Simple access to books and other material, while a prerequisite for reading success, was not enough to make all children proficient readers, according to state-level standardized reading test scores (Hodges et al., 2019). It is not enough to simply put books in the hands of our students; we must create reading curricula and reading classrooms that encourage both motivation and engagement (Afflerbach & Harrison, 2017).

While educators can understand and try to restore motivation and engagement as individual constructs, they have a reciprocal relationship and influence each other. Students' motivation to read is affected by their prior engagement. In turn, successful engagement motivates more reading. Self-efficacy, the belief in the ability to be successful, and metacognition, the ability to monitor meaning as it is constructed, also come into play when addressing motivation and engagement.

However, fostering motivation and engagement means removing commonplace rewards, reading logs, book reports, and other practices that insidiously foster educational compliance. Yet Ms. Morgan, the literacy coach, and the librarian found that tradition is hard to break. Depending on the number of minutes spent reading or number of books read, students can earn stickers, small toys, coupons for pizza or other fast-food items, gift certificates, tickets to a sporting event, movie nights, or even a chance to see their principal kiss a pig or spend the night on the school roof. Unfortunately, reading for these kinds of incentives not only doesn't encourage reading in the long term, it actually *depresses* motivation to read and diminishes the true accomplishments of reading (Marinak & Gambrell, 2016). Research proves that rewards actually don't motivate people. People are not like pets. Working *with* people to help them do a job better, learn more effectively, or acquire good values takes time, thought, effort, and courage, while doing things *to* people, such as offering them a reward, is relatively undemanding but ineffective (Kohn, 2018). After sharing the research with her cadre of teachers and parents, Ms. Morgan encouraged them to come up with ways to promote literacies without rewards, such as read-in-pajama nights, inviting therapy dogs, having the principal read aloud a book on the school's social media site every Sunday evening, or even starting intergenerational book discussion groups, like the book club whose members read about Henrietta Lacks.

Additionally, practices in literacies are not things people *do*, in that people read and write per se. Rather, engaging in restorative literacies is a nonlinear, meaningful, collaborative, political, cultural, and linguistic interaction. Interaction with texts is a social process and should be a conversation between the reader and the author, among readers, and even with oneself. In restorative literacies, interaction with texts should not be in the form of direct teaching, lectures, or assignments. Marinak and Gambrell (2016) note that relevance, access, and choice hold promise for increasing students' intrinsic motivation to read. Relevant mini-lessons, conversations, scaffolding, and practice can be used to support students in navigating the challenges and reaping the joys of reading and writing in an authentically meaningful manner. Rather than being assigned books to read, students should be invited to literature through libraries, read-alouds, and storytelling (Martinez et al., 2017). Instead of using flash cards, phonics worksheets, and multiple-choice questions; assigning book report projects; or other passive activities that focus on "getting the grade," educators practicing restorative literacies can provide the active and engaging use of a response journal, allow students to jot notes in the margins, encourage fact-checking, seek ways that students can bring up their inner activist, encourage sharing personal thoughts about books and other texts, offer personal invitations to read and present "book blessings," and ensure plenty of time to read and write.

Seeing that some of the older students in the school were still reluctant to read, the librarian at Ms. Morgan's school started writing letters to them in a notebook. The students didn't have to respond, but she knew they would at least read her letters and return their notebooks for more. She always started with a well-known quote or a short poem, and a few words to reach out to the students. One example follows:

"If you want something you've never had, you must be willing to do something you've never done."—Thomas Jefferson. Do you have any idea how amazing it is to voice strong opinions at your age? People may try to shut you down but that is on them. I'm glad you know how to stand strong in the face of adversity. Now what? You have a voice, what do you want to say? What do you want us to hear? Personally, I think you are tired of other people (mostly adults) calling the shots. I wonder if roles were reversed, how you would make decisions.—Ms. C

The restoration of positive relationships among motivation and engagement; backgrounds and perspectives; variable skills, proficiencies, and fluencies; and books and other forms of texts, and the authors of such texts, is paramount to student achievement and agency.

FOSTERING CHOICE IN READING

Too many people choose books to read based on the guidance, or potential judgment, of other people. People refer to bestseller lists or the recommendations of their friends. And if people choose a book that appears "inappropriate," they tend to read it in both deep pleasure and shame by reading it in private, changing the cover, or using ebooks or tablets. Choosing books is such a judgmentally laden process that teachers, parents, and even community members are accustomed to choosing books for their children, passing on the concept that books and other material must be chosen with utmost care. In this process, children (and adults) don't learn how to choose books independently and don't experience seeking books for different purposes. Ms. Morgan, the literacy coach, and the librarian found themselves in discussions with teachers, parents, and community members about refreshing the school library and building classroom libraries. The underlying concern of their discussions always surrounded the question of whether they trusted the children to choose books wisely or even whether the children had the ability to cope with the diverse, and perhaps controversial, information presented in books. The discussion about choosing books turned out to take place in a restorative circle, but one in which Ms. Morgan had to gently foster antiracism as the participants considered the cultural, linguistic, economic, political, and dis/ableist views of literacies.

Students should have authority over choosing books to read, and educators should say "yes" as often as they can without worrying about whether the book seems too short or too long, is too easy or too hard, or has pictures or is a graphic novel. And students should know it is absolutely appropriate to find that they don't like a particular book and to abandon it. Furthermore, if a book is beyond a student's ability, it certainly can be read aloud or shared with another person to read together (International Literacy Association & National Council of Teachers of English, 2019).

Tied in with choosing books on their own, students learn to set a purpose for reading. What are they curious about? What books are satisfying? When students' purposes for reading are clearly defined, either by themselves or during instruction by a teacher, comprehension and even their literacy skill set are greatly improved (Tovani, 2016). Students can learn to explicitly identify their purposes for reading or what information they need, instead of simply getting through a text word by word and sentence by sentence and calling it done. One of Ms. Morgan's 4th-grade teachers incorporated choice of books and articles into the students' study of the Great Lakes surrounding Michigan. One student noted that Michigan was shaped like a mitten and started seeking more metaphors about the state. Another student heard about mussels that were a threat to the ecosystem of the Great Lakes. And another student discovered that the trail behind his backyard was used long ago by Native Americans. The students were encouraged to seek a wide variety of genres to support their individual inquiry. One of the happy side effects was that the students began to get distracted at times, read other topics about the Great Lakes, and enthusiastically shared among themselves the tidbits they found.

In addition, books that people individually choose with purpose are usually connected to a person's background knowledge and with text complexity in mind. Paradoxically, comprehension of nonfiction often demands a base of prior knowledge, but reading nonfiction is also one of the ways that a base of knowledge can be built. Moreover, a broad and deep base of knowledge makes readers of fiction successful too (Lemov et al., 2016). For example, if a patient wanted to know more about a diagnosis, treatment plans, and prognosis of metastatic osteosarcoma, the knowledge would be best built up beginning with a layperson's description about metastatic osteosarcoma, such as from a pamphlet provided by a physician, before reading an oncologist's research paper filled with medical jargon. Similarly, a young student with some background knowledge of baseball, as well as the lingo that goes with the game, would be more engaged in a book about baseball and would enjoy the book more.

Ms. Morgan's teacher discovered that when students chose their own inquiry about the Great Lakes based on what they already knew, they were able to expand their literacies in surprisingly deeper ways. She remarked that even though she had a huge collection of books about Michigan and the Great Lakes, she would never go back to reading a few favorites aloud, assigning specific books to read, or her repertoire of lesson plans, worksheets, written assignments, and dioramas. Instead, she spread out her collection of books on tables for her students to browse through, helped each student think of an inquiry, and set them loose—and trusted them—to discover. And she allowed her students to share their newfound information in any way they liked, whether presenting a PowerPoint, writing a poem, demonstrating a science experiment, or making a travel brochure. Throughout the project-based learning, she provided mini-lessons and small-group instruction on such topics as recognizing text complexity, developing a good topic sentence, finding resources for spelling, and citing works. In many ways, the adults in Ms. Morgan's school began to realize that their students are a lot like themselves when figuring out what to read and why, making connections, and sharing with other people.

In restorative literacies, educators find that simply insisting that students "make inferences" while reading is ineffective (Hirsch, 2007). In fact, even the weakest reader can make inferences when watching movies, having conversations, or going on about their lives (Lemov et al., 2016). An inability to make inferences while reading is too often not an underlying cognitive disability, but a simple lack of the knowledge base for the specific texts that are given or required reading in school-like literacy. To address "issues" of knowledge, students need conceptual connections to assigned books and other texts. Lemov et al. (2016) suggested pairing texts, such as nonfiction with fiction, or books with articles, poetry, or other genres, or reading multiple texts on the same topic in order to increase absorption of new knowledge. Willingham (2017) added that other activities that promote background knowledge can include watching documentaries or videos, or conversations with knowledgeable people. Another of Ms. Morgan's 3rd-grade classrooms was learning about natural habitats as part of their science curriculum. Staff from a local raptor rehabilitation center arrived with several live owls to show the students their beaks and talons, and to share information about the owls' diets with respect to their position at the top of the food chain. The students learned that poisoning mice in turn can poison raptors, who catch the mice for their meals. Not only was there a typical presentation and discussion about raptors and their habitats, but Ms. Morgan also purchased several copies of a variety of books about owls and habitats. She encouraged one of the presenters to take a few extra minutes to read aloud a short book and to provide quick blurbs about the others. After the presenters left, the books were enthusiastically picked up and taken to individual book bins to be read during independent reading times.

When engaging in restorative literacies in schools, a promotion of rigor, relevance, relationships, and response is needed rather than just basic skills, such as reading and writing. "Books need to speak to today's readers or they will reject them as not worth reading" (Lesesne, 2010, p. 7). Lesesne defined reading ladders as a series or set of books that are related in some way and that demonstrate a gradual development from simple to more complex. The first rung of the ladder is a book that a student has already found a connection to. At each successive rung, the books, sometimes varying from genre to genre, are still reminiscent of the preceding books but are increasingly complex. Fiction can serve as a stepping stone into nonfiction, or research or a news article relating to a concept found in a novel can be used to expand understanding of plot development. Both of the teachers described above used stepping stones when inviting students to read about the Great Lakes or about owls and their habitats, successfully building motivation, engagement, and skills for reading and writing.

Assigned Readings

There are certainly times when free choice of books is not an option for students. Course curricula may require reading specific works. There are valid arguments for and against teaching canonical works. People who support the canon use these texts as a foundation, while other people challenge the texts for their Eurocentric, masculine representation of experience (Styslinger, 2017). Furthermore, textbooks for mathematics, sciences, geography, history, or other disciplinary fields must be chosen with care. When many children in a classroom are learning different, uncoordinated subject matter from different texts in the language arts curriculum, there is no practical way of ensuring that all children will gain the knowledge they need to master nationally shared knowledge (Hirsch, 2019). At the same time, not many adults have fond memories of assigned reading from their English classes, yet the one-size-fits-all class novel persists as the centerpiece of instruction (Fisher & Ivey, 2007).

Book selection committees in schools can find themselves embroiled in controversies with their communities. Ms. Morgan's school was not immune. Restorative practices and circles certainly can be used among educators, administrators, and community members during the process of selecting and assigning books for classrooms. However, this book on restorative literacies is not the place to discuss controversies on choice versus assigned readings or what books should or should not be included in the literary canon or academic field. My point in fostering choice is to promote the restorative process as a *starting point* for some of the most disfranchised readers to grow from. The goal of restorative literacies is to provide students access to material that they have clear purposes for reading, foster motivation and engagement, and improve basic reading and writing skills. In addition, practices in restorative literacies can enhance students' background knowledge in order to empower their reading comprehension (Lemov et al., 2016). Students, including those in Ms. Morgan's school, need these restorative opportunities to build up their background knowledge, make connections, develop purposes for future reading, and offer their voices and viewpoints as outlined in this chapter, regardless of whether the reading is chosen or required.

SCAFFOLDING STRATEGIC READING

In restorative literacies, everyone who reads runs into problems, such as decoding multisyllabic words (like differentiating between *etiology, ethology, etymology,* and *entomology*), confronting new vocabulary or concepts, or even finding themselves having read an entire page before realizing that it wasn't comprehended. These problems occur even with the best of choices, purposes, and personal connections. The paradox of using prior knowledge versus building a knowledge base in comprehension manifests in decoding as well. If decoding is laborious, students may refuse to read, but at the same time, reading will provide the practice and eventual proficiency and fluency. In addition, writing, an activity that challenges us to make connections, organize our thoughts, and think them through with sequence and logic, is one of the most cognitively demanding tasks that humans perform (Farrall, 2012).

The vulnerability of children, at the mercy of powerful adults as they most often are, is overwhelming (Dutro, 2019). Reading out loud and writing are particularly fraught activities in schools, to the point where some students may refuse outright invitations to read or write. Ms. Morgan and the literacy coach began to notice that it was fear, not necessarily lack of skills, that impeded some of their students' growth in literacies. When students' brains are already traumatized or fearful, from both outside and/or in-school experiences, students do not function well cognitively. When the brain perceives stress or threats, its limbic system has one of three responses: fight, flight, or freeze. Working memory, the ability to take in information, manipulate it in the mind, and come to an understanding of its significance, is constrained by negative emotion (Rodriguez & Fitzpatrick, 2014).

However, if the restorative practices of choice, purpose, and voice are in place, students who are disenfranchised readers are more likely to show a willingness to problem-solve when they are stuck on words or phrases. Most important, students are more likely to be willing to tackle challenging texts if they are in emotionally safe spaces. After all, literacy practices are the means through which life stories are encountered, shared, and witnessed in classrooms. Thus, literacy classrooms are crucial contexts for engaging the complexities of trauma (Dutro, 2019). Such trauma-informed classrooms are not only safe spaces for confronting the challenges in the process of reading and writing, but also allow for the hardest part of our personal and social lives in schools.

Students need teachers or mentors to observe, in a strength-based positive manner, what students are trying to do, but have found themselves confused about, while they are reading or writing. For example, differentiating between *etiology, ethology, etymology,* and *entomology* can be confusing, but a reader might notice the suffix *–ology* and, *if* it is in the reader's knowledge base, would know that it means a study of something. Ms. Morgan and the literacy coach saw that most often, students confronting challenging texts needed concrete strategies for untangling their confusions about words and phrases, rather than hearing adults simply correct miscues; resort to lower-level texts, phonics lessons, or worksheets; or extol the virtues of "working hard" or "developing grit."

Too often, students who are considered "struggling readers" are asked to read out loud or write under supervision. Not only might these students have performance anxiety, but the processes of reading and writing are exposed and seen as errors rather than as normal negotiations of challenges, or simple lack of knowledge, in reading and writing. During discussions about benchmarks, running records, and test scores, Ms. Morgan and her literacy coach consistently reminded their teachers and parents that reading is a nonlinear process in which readers return to miscued words and misread phrases to maintain the meaning of texts. Writing is also a nonlinear process involving brainstorming, drafting, revising, editing, and rethinking. A reading "error" in phonics also could mean an "error" in semantics. An "error" in syntax actually could be a transfer of a first language or an English variation to the English in print. An "error" in spelling could result from lack of knowledge of how a word is conventionally spelled or just from quickly jotting down thoughts. In fact, the terms *errors*, *miscues*, or *mistakes*, and especially *benchmark levels* and *red editing pens*, should not be used when working with students who are in emotionally difficult or traumatized places with their literacy development.

Instead, a restorative focus should be placed on *processes* and *meaning*. The ability to think metacognitively is further enhanced through strategies that build habits of reflection and by feedback that illuminates when strategies in reading work and when they do not (Fisher et al., 2016). The goal is to develop a self-extending system where the reader monitors their own reading and writing; searches for cues in word sequences, in meaning, and in letter sequences; cross-checks one source of cues with another and repeats as if to confirm their reading or writing; and self-corrects words (Clay, 1993). While Ms. Morgan and her literacy team worked to ensure that the school was an emotionally safe place to practice literacies, the literacy coach made it her specific goal to work closely with teachers on how to teach strategic reading in explicit and positive ways.

TIME AND SPACE FOR VOLUMINOUS READING

Thriving readers are voluminous readers when they read extensively; settle easily into personal, comfortable reading rhythms and routines; develop identity as a reader; build empathy; and enjoy discussing books with others (Harvey & Ward, 2017). All students need *time* for reading. Excellence at performing a complex task requires practice. Ten minutes a day of focused silent reading has the potential to change a student's academic life (Beers & Probst, 2017). But in some cases, the circumstances of students living in poverty or in highly stressed homes are not conducive to independent and voluminous reading. Many teachers have found that assigning reading as homework does not guarantee that reading actually will be done in homes. Proficient and fluent reading may not necessarily require the 10,000 hours that Gladwell (2008) remarked was the magic number for expertise, but the bottom line is that if students are not reading at home and they are not reading at school, they simply are not reading.

Since people's physical spaces affect their reading experiences, all students need comfortable places for positive experiences with literacies. Students need to feel like they live in, rather than just visit, the classroom spaces in which they read and write. Trusting students to find a spot that works for them and others around them, comfortable seats, and what they choose to work on at the moment goes a long way toward communicating that they are a living, breathing learning community (Ripp, 2017). Ms. Morgan's school personnel and parents were thrilled that the district prioritized funds for upgrading the rows of desks and chairs to a large set of flexible seating arrangements that included chairs, stools, modular tables, standing tables, and even yoga balls, beanbag chairs, and papasan chairs.

Using restorative literacies with a well-stocked classroom library, enthusiastic invitations to read and write, choices of books, purposes for reading and writing, scaffolded strategies, plenty of time, and comfortable spaces, students can begin to build their resilience and stamina as humane and literate beings. It was not long before Ms. Morgan found some of the most reluctant readers walking down hallways with their noses in books. She began to hear from parents reporting that their children loved to read at home without being asked or bribed. And the vocal insistence on implementing phonics instruction, while indeed an essential component, as the easy, one-size-fits-all approach to teaching reading began to simmer down. In addition to restoring relationships between people, literacies, and authors, restorative literacies also must begin to repair the harm already done in schools.

CHAPTER 6

Repairing Harm

Ms. Walker was determined. She had a "tough class" one year. Her literacy intervention class was full of 8th-graders, most of whom were assessed to be reading at a 2nd- or 3rd-grade level. The 11 students in this class, all Black or Brown boys, were out of control, feeding off one another. None of them listened. None of them would put their cell phones away in their backpacks. None of them were willing to read or write. Instead, they pushed one another around, made wisecracks, and munched on their snacks, leaving the wrappers on the floor. Some left the room and never returned. Others holed up in corners of the room playing video games on their tablets or laptops. At the advice of her principal, who was new to the school that year, Ms. Walker set up a behavior management system. She wrote each of the boys' names on the whiteboard and warned them that if someone got five check marks for misbehavior in a session, he would be sent to the principal's office. But her students seemed to manage to get just three or four check marks each and then go sit down at a desk, pull their hoodies over their heads, and lay their heads down quietly for the remainder of the class hour. Ms. Walker said this was a class she dreaded every day and was relieved when the bell rang.

There were 11 unheard stories in this class. Seeing that her students refused to read or write, possibly because they *couldn't* read or write, Ms. Walker asked the administration to purchase numerous evidence-based remedial reading programs, both workbooks and online, to try with this group of students. And when the administration refused, citing budget concerns, she purchased them herself. Ms. Walker also resorted to websites and downloaded worksheets, which she printed and stapled together to make booklets. One such booklet contained 12 pages of worksheets on turning short-vowel words to long-vowel words by adding a silent *e*, such as *cub* to *cube*, *bit* to *bite*, *tap* to *tape*, *kit* to *kite*, and *pan* to *pane*. Each page contained an assortment of illustrations, such as cute bear cubs and colorful flying kites. Ms. Walker tried following one reading remediation program after another, programs that emphasized phonics instruction or programs that emphasized whole literature; programs for struggling readers and programs that were supposed to excite readers. And even programs that came with your-money-back guarantees to improve reading skills, but none did in her classroom. To Ms. Walker's frustration, this was one wild and unruly bunch.

Since none of the remedial reading programs were working, Ms. Walker surmised that the behavior and lack of motivation of these students were the problem, not the various literacy curricula she was trying to offer. When she finally opened up about her frustrations to a colleague, Ms. Walker was told that the principal's behavior management plan was not a *positive* behavior system. Instead of check marks that would get students sent to the principal's office, she should try using stars for students to work toward a reward at the end of the class or at the end of the week. Ms. Walker didn't need even a week to find that a positive behavior system wouldn't work either. At first, Ms. Walker had not realized the complex interrelationships between cultural, linguistic, economic, political, and dis/ableist views of literacies, and the cognitive and metacognitive processes of reading proficiency, fluency, and comprehension, and writing encoding and effectiveness. Fortunately, Ms. Walker did not give up and she began a serendipitous journey of restorative literacies practices, a journey that soon became intentional, effective, and transformative.

DISMANTLING LABELS AND CATEGORIES

All 11 students in Ms. Walker's literacy intervention class did everything and anything but attend to the reading and writing assignments at hand. Ms. Walker struggled to find remedial reading programs for her students, and she struggled with trying various systems of behavior management. As was the case in Ms. Walker's "tough class," the presence of retributive justice, a form of criminal justice in our society that focuses on punishment with respect to the severity of the crime, manifests itself in classrooms as well. Also in common with the larger society, classrooms reflect distributive justice through the widespread use of therapeutic remedial reading programs or intervention classes.

However, Ms. Walker alone was not culpable for the climate of retributive or distributive justice in schools. The institutional and systemic practices of testing, ability grouping, tracking, and even institutionalized racism were responsible for the nature of the intervention class that Ms. Walker happened to be assigned to teach. Even if Ms. Walker's students were not entirely deserving of "punishment," the institutional and structural *system* saw them as needing remediation and management. The *system* also began to see Ms. Walker as an ineffective teacher with this class and in need of direct supervision by her new principal, who decided that these students needed a behavior management plan. Furthermore, the *system* allowed the administration to determine what literacy curriculum and materials were needed or not needed in this classroom. Therefore, all the people involved in Ms. Walker's intervention class needed restorative care toward re-storying the difficult educational trajectory of these 11 students of color.

Retribution in the larger society is consequential, punitive, judgmental, intolerant, and exclusionary. Retribution can both result in and result from a school culture that fosters labels and categories for students and groups of students, which in turn give rise to distributive justice. For the 11 young men in Ms. Walker's intervention classroom, the school-to-prison pipeline was a real concern. Therefore, these students not only needed restored relationships, but also needed the harm they had experienced to be repaired.

Students are widely labeled on and grouped by a spectrum from *exceptionally gifted* to *severely learning disabled*. Some students declare that they are a *level J* or a *level Q*, benchmark levels that define them as readers. Some students see themselves as a *smart student* or a *geek*. Other students define themselves as *dyslexic* or *learning disabled* and declare that they are unable to or won't read. Some students seem to take pride in being the *class clown*, and others announce themselves as participants in the *low class* or as a *bad speller*. Furthermore, the use of the term *achievement gap* perpetuates the nature of deficit systems that created it in the first place (A. Johnson, 2019; Milner, 2010). Even students as young as kindergarten or 1st grade can begin to position and label themselves in positive or negative ways. Thus, by the time students reach a middle school classroom like Ms. Walker's intervention class, these labels based on isolated skills or personal traits have become deeply entrenched in their identities as students.

When one of the students, named Darian, in Ms. Walker's class angrily remarked that he was a *nontraditional student* and wanted to go to an *alternative high school* the following year, Ms. Walker paused. She heard these terms as quite loaded coming from a middle school student in her intervention classroom. But then she noticed that her students carried all kinds of other labels for themselves. Ms. Walker realized that her first step was to dismantle and disrupt negative labels and categories. She decided that her first goal was to help her students, and the community of educators around the students, begin to see themselves as *readers* and *writers*.

Without entirely realizing that Darian, the nontraditional student, and his friend Mike, the class clown, were leading a spontaneous restorative circle about being a "nontraditional student" during class one day, Ms. Walker allowed herself to just watch and listen for the rest of the hour without making an effort to teach a lesson or control the class. She listened as the students wholeheartedly discussed their various labels and categories over their short lifespans, their current disillusionments, and their hopes for their futures. Ms. Walker even found herself labeled by some of the students as a *sweet teacher* who *lets them get away with not having to work*. Most important, Ms. Walker noticed that during this discussion, which was, unbeknownst to her at the time, a restorative circle, no one was talking out of turn, throwing punches, playing video games on their cell phones, or leaving the room. Her students may have been sitting on tops of desks or standing around, but ultimately a huddle naturally formed. Camaraderie, connections, and relationships were appearing before Ms. Walker's eyes that she had not seen before.

Jenifer Fox (2008) notes that Western education has its roots in Aristotelian logic, which is based on categorical thinking. Students are taught that learning is the process of sorting and naming things and that we divide bodies of knowledge into neat subject-matter categories, such as math, science, civics, or literature. Fox adds that, unfortunately, the concept of disability can "create" disabled students and that the growing industry around labeling and treating students with learning disabilities should be everyone's concern. Viewing students' "defiant" behavior as a symptom of a "disorder" that needs to be "managed," or perhaps even eliminated with medication, rather than a form of communication, fails to recognize students as unique individuals with their own thoughts, feelings, and needs (Gold, 2016). Too often, students who are given a label, such as disabled learner, struggling reader, or at-risk student, are shipped off to one programmatic intervention after another, and thus are deprived of the potent and meaningful literacy experiences that spring from a robust classroom community (Harvey & Ward, 2017). The conceptualization and operation of labels and categories was the very place where Ms. Walker and her students found themselves.

Furthermore, some students were not reading well, not because of intrinsic "disabilities," but because of harm done to their literacy trajectories in schools. Some students were thoroughly indoctrinated in a bottom-up approach that emphasizes mastery of specific skills and subskills, moving from small units such as alphabetic letters to bigger units such as words, phrases, and sentences, with the idea that the ability to decode can be applied to context and the act of reading later. Therefore, students may come to define reading "well" as being able to recognize words or answer questions at the end of the story, rather than reading to visualize, reflect, and respond (Wilhelm, 2016). But Ms. Walker's students *were* able to read. They read media on their cell phones, read and sent text messages, and read books outside school. They just didn't "test" well and ended up in an intervention class where their expectations were lower and their behaviors were problematic, and even more isolated reading and writing skills were emphasized.

After trying several unsuccessful remedial reading programs and attending several workshops on culturally responsive teaching, Ms. Walker recognized that one of the underlying causes of her students' disengagement was the institutionally, structurally, and socially acceptable approaches to remediating reading and writing by using programs that were not well matched to the needs of her 11 middle school males of color. She also began to see that while it is necessary to value decoding skills as an important piece of literacy learning, it is equally important to understand that the terms *decoding* and *reading* are not synonymous (Lipp & Johnson, 2019). Materials that support decoding in isolation, such as the stapled-together booklets Ms.

Walker had created with consonant–vowel–consonant words and turning short vowels to long vowels by adding a silent *e*, omit the critical component of comprehending the meaning in text. Too often, cognitive views and sociocultural views of reading are separated, with educators focusing on one or the other but not both (Cartwright & Duke, 2019). Ms. Walker also came to see that "in the head" processes, such as basic decoding and comprehension skills, can be situated in a place, with real texts and real purposes.

Once Ms. Walker was thinking about both the cognitive processes of reading *and* the sociocultural views of reading, she was galvanized to repair the harm done to her students and seek positive ways to change the direction of her class. While at the time Ms. Walker was not able to change the fact that there were 11 males of color separated from the school's general English language arts classrooms, she decided that an intervention on intervention was a place to start (Harvey & Ward, 2017). Instead of seeking reading programs and behavior management plans, Ms. Walker looked for plenty of diverse books for her students to choose from. She also incorporated the use of technology and media, and she began a routine of independent reading. Effective independent reading practices include time for students to read, access to books that represent a wide range of characters and experiences, and mutual support within a reading community that includes teachers and students (National Council of Teachers of English, 2019). Ms. Walker began her class each day with brief mini-lessons, using a mentor text on strategies, skills, elements, processes, and comprehension, such as determining the meaning of an unknown word, putting thought into character development in a fictional story, or noticing elements of structure in written pieces. Ms. Walker provided each of her students with a journal in which to write responses after reading pages of their chosen books, jot down notes on the processes of literacies, or even scribble or doodle thoughts and ideas. But Ms. Walker needed something more and realized the answer was right there in front of her: restorative circles.

GROUPS AND CIRCLES

After observing the spontaneous huddle in her classroom, Ms. Walker approached Darian and Mike to thank them for leading the discussion about labels and categories. Mike was apologetic for his rudeness and disrupting the class, but at the same time appreciative of the opportunity to regroup with his peers. However, he offhandedly remarked that he was leading a restorative circle, a practice he and some of his peers learned at a local teen zone. The circle process provides students an opportunity to speak, listen, and reflect to one another in an atmosphere of safety, decorum, and equality, allowing students to tell their stories and offer their own perspectives.

Restorative circles can be used proactively to develop relationships and build community, or reactively to respond to wrongdoing, conflicts, and problems (Wachtel, 2013). Restorative circles are not the sole means for creating a restorative environment, but can be done within the context of restorative practices in schools (Wachtel, 2013; Winn et al., 2019). Restorative circles certainly can be used when embracing both the cognitive processes, such as decoding and comprehension, and the cultural, linguistic, economic, political, and dis/ableist views of literacies.

Many pedagogical variations of literature groups and circles exist in education from kindergarten through high school. While all groups and circles can involve literacies, some are philosophical in nature and others are more instructional. Some are in small groups or may be an entire class. Some discussions are led by a teacher, and others are facilitated equally among students using either teacher-chosen or student-chosen texts or themes. Some groups and circles have an emphasis on inquiry, and others have specified instructional goals.

However, groups and circles set themselves apart from traditional teacher lectures, independent practice, and assessments. Ms. Walker was struggling with how to reach her students using a combination of whole-class activities and small-group instruction. Modern education appears obsessed with answers, both correct and incorrect, but it is the questions that drive the human mind in critical thought (Copeland, 2005). Valued conversations give us pause, slow us down, and require the best of us (Herr, 2018). Evidence has accumulated that learning occurs in interaction with others, where students engage in discursive processes that include actively processing what others have to say, challenging their perspectives, and interpreting and explaining what is being discussed (Gillies, 2014). Most notably, "academic conversations teach us wonder, tolerance, humility, and the important fact that the world is bigger than our backyard" (Miranda & Herr, 2018, p. xiii).

The various groups and circles, such as book clubs, literature circles, guided-reading groups, or Socratic seminars, can contain similar characteristics and discussion processes. However, to understand restorative literacies circles, the pedagogical distinctions between the types of groups and circles must be made.

Guided-Reading Groups

Most common in elementary schools, guided-reading groups provide a context where teachers support each reader's development of effective strategies for processing texts at increasingly challenging levels of difficulty (Fountas & Pinnell, 1996). In guided reading, the teacher groups students by their similar reading processes and their ability to read at similar text levels. The teacher carefully chooses a text and plans instruction for each guided-reading group. Depending on the needs of the groups, some teachers may emphasize a "book club" structure where students discuss comprehension, while other teachers emphasize cognitive processes of decoding words and sentences. Despite the variations, guided-reading groups tend to be sorted by abilities and/or levels, while also lacking individual choice of texts so that explicit instruction and scaffolding in reading can occur.

Socratic Seminars

Socratic seminars, usually done in a circle, are more common in secondary education, particularly in Advanced Placement classrooms. A Socratic seminar is a "systemic process for examining the ideas, questions, and answers that form the basis of human belief" (Copeland, 2005, p. 7) and "focuses the attention of all students within a class on one, typically teacher-selected, piece of text" (p. 10). Unlike a debate where opposing arguments are weighed against one another, Socratic seminars help members to understand a text deeply by linking it to other ideas and values (Fisher et al., 2016). While there are many modifications and adaptations of Socratic seminars in schools, traditional Socratic education is faulted for funneling leading questions toward discovering a predetermined truth, while appearing to allow students to think for themselves (Fisher et al., 2016; Fullam, 2015; Israel, 2002). But Fullam notes that nothing is documented in the educational literature that includes a strategy of using leading questions in contemporary educational practice. Like guided-reading groups, courses labeled as Socratic focus on a selected group of texts (often considered canonical) (Miranda & Herr, 2018), and most such courses are planned and led by adults (Israel, 2002).

Reading Groups and Book Clubs

Reading groups (or book clubs) describe a collective that meets regularly to discuss a book that all members have (or should have) read. Reading groups, ranging from more organized groups in libraries to those among close-knit friends in homes, can be as varied as the books they read. Some groups even compare books with other books or read different books with a similar theme or topic. There is usually very little discussion about the cognitive processes of reading other than perhaps a mention of a structure or style of the text or unfamiliar words. Reading groups, away from academic or literary contexts, are spaces where the talk involves informality, friendliness, and even amicable disagreement (Peplow, 2016). Less formal chats about reading and books occur spontaneously around the supper table, in kitchens, and on neighborhood walks with friends and family. While some chats involve reminiscing about memorable books from childhood or high school, some people also try to reminisce about how they learned to read as a young child or how they were reluctant to read *Beowulf* (but still got a passing grade in the class). Reading groups or book clubs can be restorative in many cases, but they tend to contain like-minded friends or members with a text chosen by a leader or by consensus.

In schools, however, there is a tendency to group students by their problems and needs, such as by students' benchmark levels or other test scores, the isolated skills needing remediation (phonics, vocabulary, or comprehension), the type of their disabilities, or the ability to control their behavior. Ms. Walker's intervention class was a result of this sorting and grouping. Contrary to what well-meaning educators hope, there is no evidence to suggest that ability-grouping practices, within classes or between classes, yield breakthrough results (Fisher et al., 2016). By segregating the problem students, schools stigmatize them. In effect, schools are saying that these students are not part of the larger school community, when what schools really want to do is to integrate them, let them know they matter (Costello et al., 2019a).

The Process of Circling

While there are many means to creating restorative environments for literacies, circles have structure, purpose, and focus (Costello et al., 2019a). A class or a group of students coming from diverse backgrounds, having diverse abilities, and bringing diverse perspectives, meet in a circle—a shape implying community, connection, inclusion, fairness, equality, and wholeness (Costello et al., 2019a). A circle may be proactive or responsive on any topic—personal, cultural, linguistic, racial, and even academic—and connected to multiple forms of literacies. The processes of circling are varied and may include using a talking stick, centerpieces or texts, or even an inner circle of participants and an outer circle of observers. And circling certainly can be used to explore the backgrounds and perspectives, as well as the variable skills, proficiencies, and fluencies, of readers. They also can explore the multiple texts readers encounter and the authors of such texts, as well as the cognitive and metacognitive processes of reading proficiency, fluency and comprehension, and writing encoding and effectiveness.

At first, some students may be unused to the democratic processes of circling, as opposed to disciplinarian and authoritarian processes of traditional teaching. But teachers who use circles on a day-to-day basis advance curricular goals, while at the same time building social capital. Even though there are increasing demands on teachers in the face of standards and standardized testing, judicious use of circles surrounding literacies (including listening, speaking, reading, writing, and reflecting) provides more time, not less, for teaching and learning, and makes for a better, more productive learning environment (Costello et al., 2019a).

Even though restorative circles most often are seen as useful for disciplinary and justice purposes, Ms. Walker came to see how the literacies and discipline in her intervention classroom were tightly interrelated and recip-rocal. She began to integrate cognitive processes of reading and writing and elements of literacies, as well as curricular standards for English language arts, into her restorative circles. At times, she opened with a quote, poem, or song. Other times, she incorporated writing such as on strips of paper, sticky notes, or a large sheet of butcher paper (Winn et al., 2019). However, what distinguishes restorative literacies circles from book clubs, literature circles, guided-reading groups, or Socratic seminars is to keep in mind what the classroom community and individuals need in terms of acknowledgment, wholeness, belonging, curiosity, and learning. In circles, even teachers, dis-ciplinarians, administration, staff, and parents express themselves. They cultivate empathy and influence behavior in ways they rarely do otherwise (Costello et al., 2019a). Restorative circles offer opportunities for choice, inquiry, self-discovery, connection, relationships, and, most of all, shared stories and re-storying.

When using diverse circles in restorative literacies, educators and stu-dents learn to see that *all* readers are challenged at one time or another. All readers run into unknown words, confront complex texts, and get stumped at times. And all readers can reap benefits from reading, gaining new knowl-edge, identifying with characters, and building capacity for empathy. All readers can develop opinions, reshape their worldviews, and refine their core values. At the same time as Ms. Walker started to campaign for full inclusion of her students in English language arts classrooms, she also kept a short list of literacy practices that came up, did a quick mini-lesson on each topic, and initiated restorative literacies circles with success in engaging and empowering her 11 students.

CHARACTERS IN A RESTORATIVE CIRCLE

Mike remarked that he couldn't keep track of all the characters in a real-istic fiction book about police brutality (Thomas, 2017). He understood that there was a Black girl who lived in a poor neighborhood but attended an affluent, predominantly White school, and that there was a party. Mike didn't quite catch the girl's name because she was the narrator in the novel. Mike also was confused about a brother in the story who was called a num-ber, Seven, and wondered whether that was a real name or a nickname. It would seem reasonable for educators to respond to Mike's remark by pre-senting a "lesson" about multiple characters and their various roles in the story, such as a protagonist, antagonist, or supporting character. It would be simple for educators to pull out a worksheet that required students to write down the names, roles, and descriptions of the characters from the book in a table format. It would be common practice to focus on broader "compre-hension skills" and list elements of stories, including settings, characters, problem, events, and solutions. Yet pulling out worksheets and lessons is in effect a remediation of "school-like" literacy and risks disengaging and even disconnecting students, especially the 11 disfranchised 8th-graders in Ms. Walker's intervention class. In fact, most proficient and fluent readers employ metacognitive strategies to overcome the hurdle of getting to know characters in stories, such as reviewing the blurb on the back of the book, turning pages back to reread or scan, or deciding to keep reading with patience and letting the story continue to develop. Very rarely do readers of novels resort to tables or graphics or worksheets. Some readers may make notes in the margins or jot down some thoughts in a journal, but usually do not do so unless they are reading for research or essay purposes.

Instead of resorting to a worksheet, Ms. Walker presented a mini-lesson that was a show of empathy, a component of restorative literacies. She acknowledged that for many readers, it *is* difficult to keep track of characters at the beginning of a novel, when readers are just getting to know the characters. She also acknowledged that Mike was not alone in his frustrations, nor was there anything wrong with Mike himself or the book in his hand. In a restorative circle, other students began to chime in on their experiences with getting to know who is who, both in unfamiliar books as well as at the beginning of new movies. While the students were discussing some of the frustrations and strategies for getting to know characters, Mike started to realize that it was okay for him to be more flexible in turning pages back and forth and to keep going and see where it led him. He also realized that the name of the narrator might not be revealed until later in the story when another character mentioned the narrator by name in dialogue. As the conversation rolled on, there was discussion about how characters may grow or change as the plot develops. This made Mike decide that a single character in his book might have different identities, such as shifting between poor neighborhoods and affluent private schools, or between real names and nicknames. Finally, the conversation strayed to how the students had revealing moments in their own personal lives that changed their mindsets or character traits. The entire group of 11 students began to see themselves and the others around them as stories, stories to be told and stories to be read.

RESTORATIVE CIRCLE WITH MULTIPLE LENSES

Ms. Walker made sure that the 11 students in her intervention class were part of their schoolwide community read. Every day, she read aloud chapters from a book about three young refuges, from different time periods and continents (Gratz, 2017). One of the restorative circles that followed a chapter involved sharing multiple lenses on the issues of mass humanitarian crises and migration. Ms. Walker, in her mini-lesson, shared how individual readers might come away with different perspectives, opinions, and connections to the plights of the characters in the book. Ms. Walker reiterated that there were no "right" answers in comprehension and that there would be no quizzes for this community read. Ms. Walker pointed out that lenses on stories can come from racial, cultural, economic, political, religious, feminist, ability, or gender/sexual identity perspectives.

Using a talking stick in a sequential manner around the circle of her students, Ms. Walker encouraged each student to share their truths and the lens from which they were hearing the book on refugees. Ms. Walker hoped that quieter voices would be heard too. A student who wanted to pass was allowed to, but none did. The responses were poignant and personal. One student revealed for the first time that his family hosted another family with humanitarian visas who had a son who needed specialized medical attention from the nearby hospital. Another shared that he never gave much thought to other countries as he was so focused on surviving the poverty and violence on the very street where he lived. He wondered whether he could be a refugee within his own town or state, say, maybe having to move across town or into another city. Pondering the definition of *refugee*, in turn, made the next student wonder whether Black people could end up being refugees in another country as a result of white supremacy, police brutality, and racism. The next student, who declared he and his family were born as Americans, shared that he was admonished to "go back to where he came from," but he didn't know where that was or how to respond. He admitted to feeling angry and had to stay in full control of himself so as to not escalate the confrontation. One student remarked that he heard about eugenics, saying that it was the idea of making *perfect people*, and wondered whether that was for real or a fictionalized concept.

As the circle continued around, there were many references to the three characters in the book and the definition of the term *refugee*, and varying responses as to how the students would rewrite the stories in the book or write their own book. Afterward, Ms. Walker pointed to a collection of other books on some of the topics that had been discussed. Some of the students pulled out their cell phones or laptops to look up articles. Most students wrote personal responses in their books, drew cartoons, or made memes, and one even wrote a letter welcoming a recent immigrant to the school. No one could say that the conversations surrounding the book on refugees, and the desire to inquire or read more about the ramifications of government policies, discrimination, and mass migrations, are not literacies.

RESTORATIVE CIRCLES ON DISCIPLINARY LITERACY

Juan stormed into Ms. Walker's classroom and slammed his natural science textbook down on the center table. The rest of his classmates, still ambling in from previous classes, were stunned at Juan's outburst, as he was not normally known for emotional eruptions. Darian remarked, "Juan, not cool." Sensing that a restorative circle would be wise (as opposed to disciplinary action or even pulling Juan aside to address his outburst), Ms. Walker decided to begin her class by listening and responding to Juan. Juan complained that the night before, he read a chapter of his natural history textbook at least six times, over and over again, but he still failed the quiz on that chapter. Ms. Walker acknowledged his frustration and asked whether anyone else in the group wanted to share their own experiences. None of the students in the intervention classroom had had successes with quizzes and tests. One student even boldly exclaimed that that was the purpose of quizzes—to keep the "dumb ones down and out." This student was not alone in his sentiments. Kendi (2019) remarks that the use of standardized tests to measure aptitude and intelligence is one of the most effective racist policies ever devised to degrade Black minds. Kendi continues that the acceptance of an academic achievement gap is just the latest method of reinforcing the oldest racist idea: Black intellectual inferiority. But Juan wanted to eventually graduate from high school so he could get a good job. And Juan knew that taking and passing science classes, along with mathematics, literature, and history, was part of the deal.

The discussion about quizzes was feisty, filled with frustrated empathy for Juan. When the students were all talked out, they realized they had forgotten that Ms. Morgan was in the room with them. Darian, ever the thoughtful student, began to apologize profusely for their harsh words about quizzes and tests. He admitted that quizzes and tests were probably necessary for making sure that students were learning stuff at school. But Juan insisted that he worked hard to get the quiz right. After all, he had read the chapter at least six times, and he felt like he was being tricked.

Ms. Morgan thanked her group for their brutal honesty about testing and shared that one of the hardest parts of teaching is finding or developing quality and relevant ways to assign grades. When Ms. Morgan expressed the vulnerability of educators in response to Darian's acknowledgment that assessments were necessary to make sure students were learning, relationships were being formed. All 11 students *and* their teacher were in this together. Ms. Morgan made two offers to her students. The first was that Juan bring the quiz and the chapter back to the class the next day so that the entire group could review them with him to make sure it was a fair quiz. Ms. Walker's second offer was to provide strategies for reading texts and taking tests. She realized that if she had provided "lessons" on study skills prior to the restorative circle, the lessons would not have been well received. But by this point, her students were *eager* to resolve the issues of passing quizzes and tests.

Over the next few days, Ms. Walker and her students explored the concept of disciplinary literacies. They discussed how reading a chapter from a science textbook for school is vastly different than reading a novel for pleasure. They discussed how reading and thinking like a scientist is different from reading and thinking like a historian, a philosopher, or a mathematician. They also discussed study skills, such as highlighting, taking notes, and categorizing information, as steps toward internalizing information. From there, they discussed how crucial it is to *understand* a topic deeply in order to be able to write or talk about it, such as making short summarizations or sketches in their notes. Having come a long way from the stapled-together workbooks on short and long vowels, Ms. Morgan's students were beginning to see themselves as literate beings capable of learning. They needed to be heard in order to move forward in the challenging environment called school.

STRATEGIC READING IN RESTORATIVE CIRCLES

Ms. Walker did not neglect the cognitive processes of decoding in her restorative literacies practices. Too much of today's reading instruction leaves students with little or no voice when talking about miscues and retelling content (Moore & Seeger, 2009). Using both curricular standards and her observations, including running records and miscue analyses, of her students' reading and writing, she provided short mini-lessons and restorative circles with assurances that *all* readers, even proficient and fluent readers, struggle at points with challenging and complex texts. *All* readers come across words that are difficult to decode or whose meaning is unknown. *All* readers are aware that there are millions of words and millions of concepts to learn, and that it simply would be impossible to know them all. The conversations about miscues and retellings were as insightful for the readers who struggled the most as for those who were more proficient (Moore & Seeger, 2009).

Keeping in mind the universal challenges of reading increasingly complex texts, Ms. Walker was able to provide mini-lessons and restorative circles on morphology, including how prefixes and suffixes change the meaning of words. She was able to do a mini-lesson and a restorative circle on the conventions of dialogue, quotation marks, and descriptive verbs used in written narratives to indicate that people are speaking. She was able to do a mini-lesson and a restorative circle on the tricky world of homophones. And she was able to demonstrate, using real texts, strategies for decoding unknown words beyond just "sounding it out." The students were encouraged to jot down or sketch conventions of literacy concepts in their journals, on sticky notes, on large poster paper for the wall, or even on strips of paper to be used as bookmarks. Some of these mini-lessons and restorative circles were done with the whole class, but many were in smaller groups of two or three students based on their current curiosity about and exploration of literacies. However, all of the mini-lessons and restorative circles used the students' current books or media as mentor texts so that the lessons were in context, explicit, and authentic. But most important, all mini-lessons started with acknowledging her students' personal feelings and experiences—and ownership—in tackling their cognitive processes of reading and writing.

THOUGHTFULLY CHOOSING AND ABANDONING BOOKS

When Ms. Walker started out teaching this literacy intervention class, none of her students were willing to read or write. After hearing and learning more about restorative practices, Ms. Walker's 11 reluctant readers were reading and writing. They were engaged, motivated, and even well on their way to building flexible, adaptable, and meaningful literacy skills. And many of the students were increasing their stamina for reading up to 20 minutes a day. At times, some were even reluctant to put their books down when the time was up. However, three of the students were chronically abandoning books and media. They would pick one up, flip through, read a few pages, and put it back down only to pick another one up. They were *reading,* but they were not fully engrossed. Ms. Walker found herself a bit frustrated with her last remaining students, the last of the group who seemed the hardest to reach.

When Ms. Walker noticed her own feelings of frustration, she realized that a restorative circle was needed on this topic. But first, she paused to think about why people might give up on a book, only to pick up another, and another. Then Ms. Walker realized that she currently was reading about eight or ten books, which were scattered all over her family room, kitchen, and bedroom. There wasn't any one that she was really digging into at the time. The more she thought, she realized that she read parts of one book with short stories just before bedtime, a nonfiction book on long Sunday afternoons, a professional book while waiting for her dinner to cook, and other books, magazines, or newspapers in the short amounts of free time she had. And she realized that one has to be in the right mood for reading about certain topics at any one time.

Maybe her students had other reasons too? Ms. Walker initiated a short restorative circle about abandoning books, not just with the three students, but with her entire group. Certainly, the practice of putting a book down and choosing another would be common among all readers. While some of the students indeed remarked that they have to be *in the mood,* they also responded that some of the books in the classroom were *kind of old and outdated.* One student shared how he wanted to read the book that was currently in his hand because he was really interested in the topic, but the words and sentences were too hard and he got tired after a few moments of reading it. Thus, he picked up another book as a break. Another student said that he can never make up his mind so he reads a little of each book to decide which one to keep reading. To Ms. Walker's surprise, a student remarked that he just looks for books that have larger print, whether he likes the topic or not, revealing that he is supposed to wear glasses but doesn't have any. And chiming in, another student exclaimed that he just couldn't get comfortable reading in that classroom. He was always cold and couldn't focus, so he would just flip through and get by. Through the use of restorative practices, Ms. Walker began to realize some of the multiple underlying reasons for her students' "misbehavior" at the beginning of the year. And she took steps to respond to not only their instructional needs for literacy development, but also their needs as humans.

Restorative circles can be used any time as a proactive process, to teach from both cognitive and sociocultural viewpoints, or as a reactive process when issues come up among students. Mini-lessons can precede or be incorporated into a restorative circle. Through building positive relationships, making connections, and fostering an acceptance of diversity, restorative circles do not point to any one individual as deviant, abnormal, or needy, but still can provide access to curricular standards and foster growth in schools. Restoring relationships and repairing harm are precursors to strengthening agency.

CHAPTER 7

Strengthening Learning With Agency

Lamar was a student in 4th grade who seemed to march to the beat of his own drummer. He never misbehaved outwardly but was quietly resistant to doing his work at school, preferring to doodle instead. He often took his assignments home to have his parents and older siblings help him, and turned them in the next day. Trevor was in Lamar's class. Trevor was a student who did everything he was told, diligently completing his assignments on time. Their teacher had a surname that was difficult to spell and pronounce, so she asked to be called Ms. Kate. Lamar and Trevor both had paraprofessionals with them in Ms. Kate's class, monitoring their behavior. Yet neither Lamar nor Trevor was making adequate progress in their spontaneous writing or in their longer written projects. Ms. Kate had made her expectations clear and used explicit visible examples for writing with Lamar and Trevor in mind. She knew that writing, including thinking about structure, conventions, and skills, is a cognitively challenging task to begin with. And yet she didn't understand why Lamar and Trevor, both Black and identified as having learning disabilities, were lagging far behind their peers.

Ms. Kate had read aloud three versions of the three little pigs folktale to her class. During a compare-and-contrast discussion of the three versions, Ms. Kate used a document camera to project a Venn diagram on her dry-erase board. She also lined up the three books on the rail below her dry-erase board with their covers facing the classroom. As the students compared and contrasted the three versions of the folktale, she wrote the elements of the stories that were similar or different in the appropriate spaces of her diagram. Her students each had a worksheet with a copy of the Venn diagram as well and were instructed to input the same information on it as Ms. Kate wrote on the projection. Lamar refused outright and instead observed quietly, and Trevor copied each word dutifully along with the other students. Seeing that Lamar had not filled out his Venn diagram, Ms. Kate took a photo of her projection on the dry erase board and emailed it to Lamar's parents so that they could help Lamar fill out his worksheet at home.

The next day, Ms. Kate's assignment was to write a paragraph explaining the similarities and differences between two versions, of the students' choosing, of the folktale. After passing out another worksheet and again using the document camera, Ms. Kate used a black marker and wrote a sentence that started with, "There are similarities and differences between the book. . . ." Ms. Kate exchanged her black marker for a green one and wrote and underlined the title of the first book. She exchanged the green marker for the black marker and wrote, "and." Then she used the green marker again to write and underline the title of the second book. Ms. Kate went on to use a red marker to write sentences containing similarities, and a purple marker to write sentences containing differences. Finally, Ms. Kate used a black marker to demonstrate a conclusion. She attempted to be explicit, visible, and even multisensory in showing how sentences were to be written when comparing and contrasting two versions of the folktale. Ms. Kate was focused on effective writing skills, even with explicit directions and special education accommodations, but without considering the cultural, linguistic, economic, political, and dis/ableist views of literacies. Thus, Lamar continued to refuse to write, and Trevor dutifully copied her examples even though Ms. Kate encouraged her students to write their own versions of the paragraph. And again, Ms. Kate took a photo of her projection for Lamar's parents.

Before the end of each day, however, Ms. Kate took time to try to support Lamar's writing. Seeing that Lamar was "struggling" but still holding expectations that he would complete the assignment, she gave him the option of doing the work in the library for 20 minutes. But without anything to copy, without the books themselves, and unable to remember all of the details discussed in class, Lamar sat in the library, doodling quietly, and returned with a blank worksheet. Ms. Kate also offered Lamar a headset and tablet so he could listen to music while he wrote, in order to reduce distracting noise, but the music itself was distracting and he kept changing the songs. Finally, Ms. Kate urged Lamar to write on a tablet, using speech-to-text software, as an accommodation. But Lamar struggled to develop a Venn diagram, insert all of the elements, and make it look like what was on the projection. Lamar saw that his peers easily could copy Ms. Kate's paragraph or write a slight variation of it, and he didn't want to set himself apart by talking into a tablet to get his paragraph down.

Ms. Kate was following the curricular standards for English language arts, one of which required comparing and contrasting literature. Unfortunately, curriculum standards do not always consider the backgrounds and perspectives, as well as the variable skills, proficiencies, and fluencies, of readers and writers. Ms. Kate was keenly organized; was considered a highly effective teacher by her principals; offered differentiation, accommodations, and even a restorative circle or two; communicated well with parents; and thought that she was doing "all the right things" according to her district's norms. But her efforts still weren't working for Lamar's and Trevor's growth as writers. Restorative literacies, in an actively engaging, participatory, and empowering way, were needed, not only for Lamar and Trevor, but for the entire class.

DEEPER INCLUSION

Ms. Kate was a gifted and reflective teacher. However, as her school district was in the throes of moving toward a workshop model during literacy learning time, Ms. Kate began to think more deeply about inclusion in this new workshop model. Since a workshop model would allow students to explore on own their terms, she worried that students like Lamar and Trevor would become even more "lost." According to Lamar's parents, Lamar was "super anxious." And both Lamar and Trevor had "learning disabilities," but Ms. Kate wasn't sure what those learning disabilities were. She came to see that neither of them, despite her best efforts, was empowered to learn, and she wasn't sure that they would be able to function or collaborate well in a workshop model. For that matter, Ms. Kate began to realize that her entire class was dutifully coasting along, unchallenged, throughout the school year, completing simple tasks such as filling out diagrams and writing complete sentences.

Ms. Kate wanted her literacy instruction to foster full inclusion, empowerment, and agency, not instruction in which she added differentiation and accommodations to the standards and curriculum for just a couple of students, like Lamar and Trevor. Indeed, including students with a range of cultures, languages, and abilities can be the catalyst for building relationships, repairing harm, and transforming a classroom. Being mindful of diversity, equity, and students with disabilities as a forethought (rather an afterthought) when delivering curriculum standards helps general education teachers improve teaching and learning for everyone (Hehir, 2005; Henderson, 2011). Otherwise, students who appear to diverge from the mainstream curriculum and school routines encounter physical isolation (e.g., referrals, suspensions, and expulsions) as well as symbolic alienation (e.g., low expectations and labeling) throughout their academic trajectories (Winn, 2013). Even students with disabilities who spend a large portion of their days in a general education classroom under the guise of "inclusion" may not be fully accessing the literacy curriculum. They may have well-meaning paraprofessionals following students closely, explaining, or even doing unnecessary things. Some paraprofessionals become the teachers themselves, providing students with separate assignments at a separate table or in the hallway. Inclusion is not inclusion if students with disabilities are placed in general education in body only (Wolter, 2015).

Lamar and Trevor were both placed in Ms. Kate's general education classroom, but Ms. Kate began to question the quality, not the quantity, of their inclusion and agency despite her best efforts to provide differentiation and accommodations. At the same time that Ms. Kate was thinking about literacy instruction in a workshop format, she began to think about how restorative practices are about doing *with*, and not doing *to* or *for*. As vulnerable as Ms. Kate felt, she thought that perhaps she could learn the workshop model *and* create a different kind of inclusion *with* Lamar and Trevor.

Approaches to maintaining social norms, discipline, and behavioral boundaries can be conceptualized in four ways: (1) authoritarian, which means doing something *to* an individual or a group, including taking punitive actions; (2) paternalistic, doing something *for* an individual or group; (3) neglectful and irresponsible, which is doing *nothing* for an individual or group; and (4) mutual, democratic, and restorative, which entails doing something *with* an individual or group (Costello et al., 2019b). Ms. Kate realized that the use of her lecture, documentation camera, diagrams, and colored markers was doing *to* and *for* her students. Without a sense of agency, Lamar waited until he got home to do the work, and Trevor copied the work, both out of their duty to comply. At the same time, Ms. Kate feared that simply placing a workshop model of literacy learning in her classroom, in the manner that she originally had perceived it, would be similar to doing *nothing* for students like Lamar and Trevor, but simply sitting back and watching them explore. Once Ms. Kate let go of the perception that a literacy workshop model is not entirely permissive, she began to figure out how to develop parameters for guiding her students toward meeting curricular standards.

INQUIRY AND EQUITY

Student choice, voice, and agency, such as independent reading, shared reading, open-ended writing, and restorative literacies circles, can be powerful motivators for students and educators alike. But educators still need to cover surface skills and common curricular standards. In the face of compressed time, Ms. Kate was attempting to cover two standards at once, determining the theme of a story, drama, or poem from details in a text, and comparing and contrasting stories in the same genre on their approaches to similar themes and topics (NGA/CCSSO, 2010). At the same time, she was attempting to foster sentence structure and writing skills. Ms. Kate was committed to being concrete and explicit in her instruction for students like Lamar and Trevor; however, she wanted to move toward equity while being mindful of the cultural, linguistic, economic, political, and dis/ableist impacts of literacies in her district's workshop model.

Since the time of Socrates and Plato, people across a wide range of fields have tried to define *learning*. While current theoretical perspectives have evolved as potential foundations for effective teaching, previous studies tended to be based on the outcomes of learners, particularly in terms of awarded grades and standardized testing, rather than the learning process itself (Khalaf, 2018).

Traditional and inquiry-based learning pedagogies are the two dominant learning models of today, both having advantages and drawbacks (Khalaf, 2018). Traditional classes do not favor agency or active engagement of learners in the learning process. In traditional learning, teachers are the senders of knowledge that needs to be covered, and students are the receivers of this knowledge regardless of the limitations of the students' background knowledge. For example, Ms. Kate realized that her students were fully capable of comparing and contrasting things such as the quality of their lunches, the antics of their siblings, or the latest episode of a movie, but she needed to make this connection with the elements of folktales. Furthermore, while Ms. Kate was mindful of differentiation and accommodations for Lamar and Trevor, she was still covering the standards and skills in a traditional pedagogy.

Inquiry-Based Learning

Inquiry-based learning usually is carried out in the scientific fields and typically is situated in an annual research project, but it certainly can be used on an everyday basis while exploring literacies, literary elements, and even cognitive processes for reading and writing in the classroom (Marino & Eisenberg, 2018). Inquiry-based learning models are complex and fall under various terms, definitions, and forms, such as personalized learning, project-based learning, problem-based learning, participatory research, and even workshops. However, learning is a process, not an event (Fisher et al., 2016). And seeking information toward problem solving is more than just a Google search. Inquiry is a "process that involves identifying the need for information, determining the best resources, locating and accessing information, synthesizing and sharing information, and evaluating the process" (Marino & Eisenberg, 2018, p. 58). This process also involves elements that librarians are familiar with in their work with information literacy. Ms. Kate sought the expertise of her school librarian as the district began the move toward a workshop model in literacy instruction. While inquiry (as well as reading and writing) is an interactive, recursive, and nonlinear process, students certainly need the development of surface skills and metacognitive awareness for deeper learning and critical analyses. Lamar and Trevor may have been resistant to writing because of their learning disabilities, but at the same time they may have been resistant because of the passivity and inauthenticity of the learning processes, a vicious cycle that needed to be disrupted.

In a literacy workshop, students are motivated and engaged in authentic inquiry about topics that are relevant to them. A historically responsive literacy framework, a model that is grounded in Black literary societies of the 19th century, includes identity development, skill development, intellectual development, and criticality (Muhammad, 2020). All four areas are emphasized, not just skill development, which is so prevalent in teaching and learning. Therefore, students spend time in school doing what readers and writers do: learning to understand their physical, social, and emotional world, and growing toward being informed global citizens. They think, talk, read, and write about their world through access to a huge volume of texts that provide rich, diverse examples of genre, theme, topic, setting, and other literary qualities (Fountas & Pinnell, 2018). When Ms. Kate decided to try again, with the help of the school librarian, to cover her lesson on determining a theme and comparing and contrasting stories, she laid out multiple copies of diverse folktales, both traditional and contemporary versions, on tables around the classroom. Ms. Kate led a brief, 5-minute discussion about "shopping" for books before allowing her students to walk around and browse the tables. The eagerness among the students, even Lamar and Trevor, was immediately apparent, and it was not long before individual students or even pairs of students sat down around the classroom fully engrossed in their chosen folktale. Some students even returned their books for another one or two. After 20 minutes of reading, Ms. Kate regrouped the students in a brief restorative circle to discuss the genre of folktales, identify themes, and acknowledge the diverse folktales that strayed from traditional versions.

The next day, Ms. Kate held another "shopping" session, but this time she asked her students to choose one book they each would use as their own anchor book for the lesson on comparing and contrasting versions of folktales. She also asked them to each find a buddy or two. Ms. Kate presented a quick reminder of how to put together a Venn diagram and provided each pair or group of students a large piece of butcher paper and a set of markers. She asked them either to read their anchor books to their partners or to swap books and read independently. Then the students were to discuss and sort out the similarities and differences between their books. Ms. Kate noticed that all of her students, including Lamar and Trevor, were quickly and eagerly participating and fully engaged in choosing books, comparing their books with peers, and putting together Venn diagrams. Instead of being at the front of the class presenting her material, Ms. Kate circulated around the classroom providing guidance, mini-conferences, and access to strategies and tools. And instead of her two paraprofessionals sitting next to "difficult students" like Lamar and Trevor, monitoring their behaviors, the paraprofessionals found themselves engaged and exploring *with* Lamar, Trevor, and their buddies. Both Ms. Kate and her paraprofessionals found themselves doing things *with* their students, instead of *to, for,* or *not at all.*

When it was time to move on to writing a paragraph, Ms. Kate presented a short mini-lesson on structuring a paragraph, but then allowed ample time for her students to practice writing their own paragraphs based on the information from the Venn diagrams they had put together on the butcher paper. Ms. Kate's students had opportunities to interact with one another as they wrote their paragraphs, providing suggestions, feedback, and edits.

Simple coverage in traditional teaching requires compliance, even with differentiation and accommodations, but inquiry allows room for motivation, engagement, active learning, and agency. At the same time, a few moments of traditional teaching are necessary, such as explaining how to develop a Venn diagram or good sentence structures. When both traditional teaching and inquiry are carefully situated, curricular standards and surface skills certainly can be taught and practiced in a workshop model.

ACTIVE LEARNING AND AGENCY

Traditional learning produces active and nonactive learners, but inquiry-based models combine both learning and practice (Khalaf, 2018). Inquiry-based learning allows room for acknowledging backgrounds and perspectives, developing cognitive and metacognitive processes, and increasing the variable skills, proficiencies, fluencies, and effectiveness of reading and writing. Not only can a curricular shift foster active learning, but school cultures that foster trust and draw on the strengths of communities contribute to the development of young people's sense of agency and belonging (Riley, 2019). A shift in curricular delivery, along with a school culture of relationships and trust, is necessary for restorative literacies.

When inquiry-based models are merged with restorative literacies, both educator and student agency are cultivated. Agency is the ability to manage one's learning, co-occurring with choice and voice in classroom settings. Agency in restorative literacies can foster engaging and voluminous reading and writing opportunities. The concept of agency is situated in the history of religion, philosophy, ethics, and law out of a need for legal, ethical, moral, and practical notions of human responsibility (Matusov et al., 2016). However, Matusov et al. note that in education there is a focus on owning and determining the endpoints of learning. While normative views of agency are conceptually mapped and emphasized, there is no one "correct" definition of agency. For example, Lamar's resistance and Trevor's compliance are certainly forms of agency, but they do not contribute to the kinds of growth necessary for building writing skills. However, the non-normative forms of agency, such as resistance and compliance, can be agentic, powerful, and informative to educators.

When students in a dynamic community that values the richness of linguistic, ethnic, and cultural diversity believe in their ability to acquire and use language and literacy for meaningful purposes, the students act as powerful agents in their own learning (Fountas & Pinnell, 2018). The relationship between structure and agency is a perennial sociological question (Rigby et al., 2016). Structures in schools are patterns that can both enable and constrain individual actions, whereas agency describes situated practices and the capacity for individuals to take action. Agency in restorative literacies is not just about a student's reading motivation, interest, or engagement, but about how these dimensions interact to open up new learning opportunities. Agency cannot be conceptualized solely at the individual level because students position themselves and are positioned within a classroom context that can either support or detract from their ability to exert influence during their learning (Vaughn et al., 2020). Ms. Kate was wise to think about what she could do *with* Lamar, Trevor, and the rest of their class instead of focusing on deficits such as "learning disabilities" and a supposed intrinsic inability to achieve growth in writing. Ms. Kate positioned herself to see her students' choices and hear their voices as they navigated through reading folktales, inputting Venn diagrams, and writing paragraphs.

Literacy is not just an individual cognitive process, but is also socially constructed. Feedback from the teacher and peers has a powerful impact on student literacy learning, placing it in the top 10 influences on achievement (Fisher et al., 2016). Timely, specific, understandable, and actionable feedback provides information that students need in order to move incrementally toward successes, and it should be offered prior to, not after, summative assignments. Targeted feedback focuses specifically on helping students build or refine a certain skill, such as punctuation (commas, colons, semicolons, and dashes), in a short piece (M. Johnson, 2020). Thus, targeted feedback is clear, goal-oriented, meaningful, and timely. Furthermore, papers are not overloaded with a teacher's pen, which can overwhelm students, nor are they used as a summative assessment. Feedback is heard when there are restorative and trusting relationships between the reader, the text, and the educator.

Given human beings' propensity for storytelling, agency can be seen as a restorative form of story and re-storying. Stories told about ourselves to other people and to ourselves shape who we think we are. Therefore, educators need to look at the kinds of stories we arrange for students to tell themselves (A. Johnson, 2019). Teacher conversation with students like Lamar and Trevor—such as asking, "What can you do?" or "How can you do this?"—guides students toward building bridges between action and consequences, bridges that develop their sense of agency. Restorative literacies use pedagogical neutrality in that educators should not tell students what is right or wrong. Instead, educators should encourage them to think about each issue critically and listen carefully to opposing views. If educators do this, instead of expecting students to believe and memorize, the material comes alive and students see the point of studying it (Noddings & Brooks, 2016). In other words, educators should let students tell their own narratives about their literacies and learning.

We currently are moving away from a skill- and knowledge-based economy toward an agency-based economy. Agency-based participation and education bring meaningfulness, excitement, and humanity, while standards-based participation and education bring alienation, boredom, and exploitation (Matusov et al., 2016). Agency and authenticity can tie together the cultural, linguistic, economic, political, and dis/ableist views of literacies, as well as the variable skills, proficiencies, and fluencies of readers; the multiple texts readers encounter; and the authors of those texts. Making shifts in pedagogy that foster a community of active participants and learners, and move away from a climate of compliance and testing, is a dynamic, diverse, and inclusive endeavor. Active learning, along with choice, voice, feedback, and interaction, can encompass both cognitive and sociocultural views of literacy development, as well as both coverage of curricular standards and a sense of agency. Then, and only then, can schools become a space where students can not only meet expectations but also thrive. Restoring relationships, repairing harm, and strengthening agency lead to another form of agency in literacies: leadership.

CHAPTER 8

Developing Leadership and Sustainability

Aaron was ticked off. Normally an easygoing 10th-grader with an endearing smile from ear to ear, Aaron suddenly exploded with anger. In the middle of an English lesson on sentence structure, he peeked at his phone and read that arming teachers was being bandied about as a solution to prevent mass shootings after a gunman in a Parkland, Florida, high school killed 17 students and staff members and injured 17 others. Aaron stood up and yelled that if we arm our White teachers, he wasn't going to come to school anymore. Aaron admitted that while there was "stuff" going on in his school—meaning that he and some of his peers were prone to apathy, defiance, and disruption—school, unlike the streets, was still a safe haven —a place to goof off and even learn something without worrying about being shot.

Aaron had the mass shooting on his mind instead of the lesson on the structure of sentences. Even though Aaron's classmates had variable levels of proficiency, fluency, and effectiveness in their reading and writing skills, Aaron's teacher was following a prescribed lesson plan with fidelity. It was a dry lesson plan taken from a teacher's manual, without containing cultural, linguistic, economic, political, and dis/ableist views of literacies. Aaron's English teacher, Ms. Powell, droned on at the front of the class during this explicitly structured lesson, but no one was listening.

Here was an opportunity for more stories. There were many stories in the aftermath of the Parkland tragedy—stories in the form of emotional pleas, listening sessions, and student protests and walkouts. There were stories of youth emerging as leaders in the national spotlight. Indeed, stories in the form of news articles, viral videos, and memes were circulating around in Aaron's classroom—some whispered among classmates and many read furtively from cell phones under tables. Most of the students in Aaron's class were paying little or no attention to Ms. Powell, who was demonstrating on the whiteboard how sentences contain nouns, adjectives, and verbs.

Although Aaron's story needed to be heard, Ms. Powell, who was White, was startled and aghast at Aaron's torrent of words. Her story needed to be heard too. It wasn't her idea to arm teachers. As a matter of fact, she previously had remarked to her friends and family that if our country came down to arming teachers, she was going to quit teaching. But Ms. Powell hadn't planned to take her lesson plans in a different direction because of the incident in Parkland. She thought that the consistency and stability in her day-to-day lessons were most needed at a time of national crisis. The silence in the classroom after Aaron's brief outburst was deafening.

Ms. Powell, frightened, asked a special education teacher, Ms. Edwards, what she should do to respond to both her students' inattention to her lessons and to Aaron's "misbehavior" that week. Ms. Edwards had known Aaron since he was in middle school. Aaron was a tall, athletic, friendly, and caring person. He had always stayed out of trouble, respected his parents, and watched out for his younger siblings, cousins, and the neighborhood children. As Aaron was coming of age and becoming something of a role model, he was also becoming increasingly outspoken about social and political issues impacting him and his friends, particularly after he found out that he had an IEP and that the English class with Ms. Powell was for special education and intervention students. He was furious because all of his peers in that class were Black, and he made it clear to Ms. Edwards that being Black was not a disability. He wanted her to show him where the White students were and what they were doing during while he was in his English class with Ms. Powell. Unfortunately, as Aaron was becoming more aware of and vocal about racial inequity and social justice, he suddenly was finding himself in more trouble in school. Thus, Aaron's worried parents, knowing that Aaron's reading levels were "below grade level," asked their pastor, the school principal, and Aaron's school counselor for guidance. Aaron's parents kept pleading with Aaron to stay on course so he could graduate. Restorative literacies were needed to see where Aaron's "troubles" were coming from and how he and his school could respond to the kinds of literacies, such as reading on his cell phone about arming teachers, that Aaron pursued.

DEFINING LEADERSHIP

Educators can misidentify acts of leadership among students as problem behaviors. In prioritizing classroom tranquility and curricular standards, educators inadvertently may be discouraging the development of characteristics of leadership, such as rule-breaking or boisterousness, in young people. How could Aaron's emerging leadership abilities, and his increasing vocalizations about injustices, be seen as an asset to his school and community instead of a liability or a challenge? If educators mistake leadership behaviors for problem behaviors, or if they do not understand the importance of nurturing such behaviors, children's leadership abilities may be thwarted (D. L. Fox et al., 2015).

Aaron and his classmates were not paying attention to Ms. Powell's lesson on sentence structure because their minds were on the recent Parkland shooting. When Aaron suddenly erupted with ire upon reading on his phone about the idea of arming teachers, Ms. Powell knew Aaron needed to be heard. Even though she didn't know how to, or even whether to, respond, she chose not to call him out on his disruption, knowing that Parkland was still a raw and sensitive issue that day. Aaron had been prone to "behavior issues" lately, but Ms. Powell didn't feel it was right to "discipline" him. It might have felt emotionally safe in the moment to drop the issue and move on with the lesson, but if she did so, Aaron would go unheard. After his outburst, Aaron retreated into his silence, along with the rest of the class, and with it, Aaron's potential for leadership was dashed.

Leadership and Student Voice

There are many definitions of leadership because leadership means different things to different people. Leadership can be a process of social influence, not necessarily by authority or power, that maximizes other people's engagement, empowerment, and identity. Leadership in the form of student voice is a concept and a set of approaches that can position students alongside credentialed educators as critics and creators of educational practice (Cook-Sather, 2020). D. L. Fox et al. (2015) note that the most prevalent student leadership characteristics involve problem solving, verbal communication skills, empathy, prominence, self-confidence, energy, flexibility, independence, responsibility, and organization. Leadership development often has been thought of as an area solely for gifted and talented students. Instead, student voice and leadership rapidly are opening up spaces and capacities for youth who historically have been marginalized on the basis of race and ethnicity to play key roles in school change (Gonzalez et al., 2017). Even though the literature dealing directly with leadership in very young children is scant (Mullarkey et al., 2005), children in pre-K through 2nd grade want to be heard, even as they are developing self-regulation skills, language expression, and their sense of agency (K. Fox, 2016). Teachers often describe children's leadership skills in positive ways in the abstract, but these theoretical beliefs quickly are challenged by the realities of managing the classroom. As a result, teachers face the complex dilemma of supporting individual children's leadership strengths while nurturing their own visions of classroom community (Mullarkey et al., 2005). Leadership and literacies are closely intertwined in attempts to merge cultural, linguistic, economic, political, and dis/ableist views of literacies with cognitive and metacognitive processes of reading proficiency, fluency, and comprehension, and writing encoding and effectiveness.

TOWARD SHARING POWER

In schools, student leadership often can be confused with voice and agency. But voice and agency without a shift toward influence, authority, or power do not promote leadership for educational and societal change. Children's lives are structured by adult views of how those lives should be lived and of what childhood should be. One approach to developing student leadership accepts the generational order, assuming the superiority of adult knowledge and the relevance of documenting or acknowledging childhood in light of adult knowledge. Another approach questions the generational order in that good information about childhood must come from children's experiences and knowledge. In the latter approach, children are taught by adults that the power issues between children and adults are diluted or defused. However, children still think otherwise, because a central characteristic of adults is that they have power over children (Mayall, 2008). After all, teaching reading and writing, along with testing of reading and writing skills, is overseen by adults who hold the power, but literacies are defined by the individual and the community.

Aaron noticed and questioned the makeup of his English special and intervention education class as predominately Black. Ms. Powell, after hearing Aaron's concern from Ms. Edwards, was open to working toward change. She too was concerned over the fact that this class was a segregated group. She also wanted to see how Aaron could participate as a leader, alongside with the educators and administrators, in changing the structure of how students are placed in their classrooms. Participation rights are very important within a societal context where adult authority and power are absolute. Children's role as citizens and their understanding and awareness of democracy are determined by the extent to which their participation rights are respected. Participation rights support a sense of belonging and inclusion. But more important, participation rights teach children how they can bring about change (Smith, 2007). The development of student agency includes creating mechanisms through which students are included in meaningful processes of analyzing teaching and learning so that their voices and perspectives inform classroom practices (Cook-Sather, 2020).

Aaron had a perspective about arming teachers beyond what he termed a "White people view of school safety." Aaron had read that some people thought that arming teachers might make schools safer, but he thought that would not make school safer for him and other young Black males. In restorative literacies, Aaron's perspective and other stories can be fully told when we see a new paradigm for what counts as literacy (A. Johnson, 2019; Kirkland, 2014). Through an expanded view of literacy, Aaron could emerge as a strong, capable, and respected leader if he had an authentic opportunity to place his energy and focus on reading and writing about a wide range of opinions and policies on school safety. And at the same time, his proficiency and fluency as a reader and effectiveness as a writer would only improve.

Educators who engage in a range of antibias, multicultural, and social justice issues, and in restorative literacies, embrace the voices and agencies of all of their students. The antibias framework offered in Teaching Tolerance (Southern Poverty Law Center, 2016) is a set of anchor standards and age-appropriate learning outcomes in identity, diversity, justice, and action. The domain of action is where students like Aaron can begin to develop leadership and offer other views of what it means to be safe in the context of school. Such actions encourage students to express empathy when people are excluded or mistreated because of their identities. Furthermore, students recognize their own responsibility to stand up to exclusion, prejudice, and injustice. Restorative literacies is a space where students, educators, and community members can begin to develop and express antibias consciousness.

OPPORTUNITIES FOR DEVELOPING LEADERSHIP

Paths to leadership, in or out of school, can take many forms. Some people lead in racial, spiritual, ethical, ecological, educational, or political ways. Aaron was speaking the language of race when he wondered why all the students in his class were Black and asked where all the White students were. He also spoke up about the ideas for preventing gun violence in schools and openly questioned how some ideas might impact the education and lives of Black students. Leadership also can shift priorities over time. Leadership, in both formal and informal settings, can be collaborative and intergenerational between students and educators in schools, or between children and adults in communities. Many modes of leadership also overlap. For example, in Aaron's community a racial issue might be addressed through the help of Aaron's pastor, an education issue with his English teacher and special educator, or a political issue through his local school board.

A plethora of self-help books and articles provide advice and tips for adults on developing leadership competencies and personalities in workplaces, organizations, and educational institutions. Hassan et al. (2016) summed up 39 leadership styles according to their key characteristics, such as autocratic, democratic, laissez-faire, charismatic, participative, ethical, authoritative, intellectual, delegative, coaching, supportive, consultative, visionary leadership, and so forth. They found that personality has an impact on the leadership style of leaders. However, Cain (2013) remarked that there is a tendency to overestimate the degree to which leaders need to be outgoing. The more a person talks, the more other group members direct their attention to that person, which means that that person becomes increasingly powerful. However, much leading is not done in front of big groups. Introverts have an inclination to listen to other people and a lack of interest in dominating social situations. In some circumstances, a quiet, modest style of leadership may be equally or more effective. Certainly, the medium of multiple literacies is an avenue for empowering leadership.

However, unlike adults, children are not always seen as leaders. Throughout the 20th century, social concerns about childhood have been caught between the ideas that children are either *in danger* or are *dangerous*. Thus, public policy responses to these two ideas have tended to zigzag as the exponents of one idea or the other gain a temporary upper hand (Prout, 2003). While Aaron's parents saw Aaron in danger of not graduating from high school, some of Aaron's teachers saw Aaron as dangerous to the status quo in the school. Too often students of all ages are seen as apathetic, too immersed in social media or video games, or in need of care and involvement in various extracurricular activities. But they simply may be unable to develop voice, agency, and leadership in myriads of ways.

Instead of continuing lessons on sentence structure using arbitrary examples from a textbook as a way of avoiding concepts of danger, such as the Parkland shooting, restorative literacies could bring out the literacy that the students were furtively reading and sharing among themselves. Through reading and sharing openly with Ms. Powell, Aaron and his classmates could begin to see that news articles, opinion pieces, and even memes all have different persuasive styles and structures. In this way, students could learn various structures while composing their own pieces in response to the Parkland tragedy. In restorative literacies, educators can reconsider children's claim on citizenship in societies.

A change in the way students are seen by educators and other adults is crucial in order for student voices to be fully heard and for agency toward student leadership and literacies to occur. Once everyone in Aaron's life— his parents, his educators, and his family pastor—began to see Aaron's impassioned concern about social and political issues impacting him and his peers as potential leadership for change, they began to see his "behavior" and his "reading" in a more positive light. After all, Aaron noticed the racial makeup of his special and intervention education class and he read and responded to news about the Parkland shooting.

Many schools offer various forms of volunteer opportunities for older students to mentor younger students as part of leadership development programs for students to gain real-world experiences. Knowing that Aaron's reading proficiency and fluency needed to improve, Aaron's special education teacher and principal tried engaging Aaron to help increase the diversity of the book collections for their reading buddies program. This program paired high school students with elementary school students to read children's books together in an informal setting, such as in a media center or outdoors on a warm, sunny day. Aaron was already reading aloud to his younger siblings, cousins, and any neighborhood children who happened to be alongside. Although Aaron originally read aloud to his siblings and cousins as part of his household chores, along with taking out the trash and emptying the dishwasher, he knew the importance of reading books to young children. Reading to his siblings and cousins came to be a task Aaron saved for the end of the day because he looked forward to reading aloud—emoting every word and making all the children around him join him in laughter. However, while Aaron found selecting books for the reading buddies program enjoyable, this was a short-term assigned leadership project, one that Aaron suspected was a disciplinary consequence of his outburst in his English classroom. In the aftermath of the Parkland violence, Aaron's church, along with many organizations across the nation, offered a youth leadership program. There were also formal opportunities, which Aaron could apply for, to represent his peers on committees and advisory boards. While Aaron's parents, educators, and pastor were attempting to identify leadership roles that would fit Aaron, Aaron's own voice about gun violence, the Black students with IEPs in the English classroom, and even his own leadership initiatives remained unheard.

Although developing critical leadership skills such as effective communication, problem solving, ethical decisionmaking, and goal-setting could help youth in navigating and solving the world's problems, a leadership program can end up being a collection of interesting leadership activities lacking an intentional and developmental approach. Many of these leadership programs offer experiences where participation alone is often the leadership development activity (Seemiller, 2018). Ms. Powell recognized the continuation of efforts among Aaron's educational and community advocates to do things *to* and *for* Aaron, rather than *with* him, in their attempts to develop his leadership competencies.

Ms. Powell took to heart Aaron's views on arming teachers and the overrepresentation of Black students in her English classroom; both were issues Ms. Powell herself was concerned about as well. At the same time, Ms. Powell wanted to develop intrapersonal, interpersonal, societal, and strategic leadership competencies (Seemiller, 2018) not only in Aaron, but also in herself for her literacy intervention classroom, and to create school-wide change. Even though Ms. Powell knew that listening to children does not mean taking all children's utterances at face value or giving their views more weight than those of adults, she saw that when children, including Aaron, become independent communicators, they are usually articulate, capable of expressing their own opinions, and able to make good choices and decisions (Smith, 2007).

A NEW COLLABORATION

Aaron most wanted to see change in his classroom and school, and not just join a leadership program like reading buddies, a youth group, a committee, or an advisory board. Mechanisms that foster student voice and student agency can focus on students working with teachers and even researchers to analyze classroom practices, engage in research through various methods, and author and coauthor texts, all with the goal of maximizing and democratizing education for everyone involved (Cook-Sather, 2020).

Ms. Powell began to collaborate with Aaron and his peers, along with Ms. Edwards, the school's special education teacher, on coming up with a new and meaningful framework of routines for their English class. Ms. Powell shared the givens—the state standards and district requirements for the coursework—and then asked Aaron and his peers to analyze the classroom practices. In this participatory research, Ms. Powell did not try to convince her students of her reasoning for what or how she taught, but rather she asked for their input on how classroom practices could be improved for them as students.

In participatory research, educators can consider the question: What does it mean to engage students, teachers, and school communities in a transformative process of democratic inquiry and meaning-making when such communities have been placed in the straitjackets of high-stakes testing and neoliberal restructuring? (Galletta & Torre, 2019). Ms. Powell didn't have the means or the time to conduct a formal participatory research project, but at Aaron's request, she listed the anonymous reading scores of the class and circled the target score on her whiteboard. Aaron and his peers analyzed the scores and discussed the controversy of high-stakes standardized testing and marginalization. One of Aaron's classmates pointed out that it was a civic imperative that as Black kids, they call out the marginalization and make sure they reach the standards. And he didn't want to graduate not having skills needed for college or a job. Aaron and his peers began to explore the ways students in general can move from their current scores to the target score. All of the students in Ms. Powell's English class rejected outright the current practices, such as lectures about sentence structure from a manual, as not working for them. In their quest for a better teaching method or program, some students looked up on their phones and tablets how to improve reading test scores. Some students discussed concerns in a small group and came up with ideas of their own. One student decided to call his aunt, who was an elementary teacher in another district. All of the students had choice in their inquiry about how reading and writing can be taught and learned.

Aaron and two of his peers chose to visit several "White" classrooms. When Aaron returned from these classrooms, he was indignant that all the students were doing at the time was reading their own individual books. Every cover looked different. Aaron remarked that you could hear a pin drop in these classrooms. Ms. Powell admitted that she knew that the first part of every general English class hour was set aside for independent reading. She was embarrassed to admit that at first she wasn't sure whether

Aaron and his peers in the special and intervention education classroom were up to the task because of their low reading scores and inattention to her lessons. Aaron was furious. He remarked that while he might have not been the best reader in the school, he read to his siblings and cousins every night, read a lot of "stuff" on his own, and was sure that his peers could read to some extent too.

Ultimately, Aaron and most of his classmates came to a consensus that independent reading and writing practice was the best way to improve their assessment scores. Ms. Powell agreed to allocate the first 15 minutes for reading, along with 5-minute quick writes in response to that day's reading, just like in the mainstream classes. Ms. Powell, Ms. Edwards, and the district coordinator gathered grant funds to purchase diverse and contemporary books and blank journals for Ms. Powell's classroom. Furthermore, since a few students were able to read and write independently but did not perceive themselves as able to do so (Williams, 2017), the district coordinator provided Ms. Powell and Ms. Edwards with coaching on differentiating instruction with respect to the cognitive and emotional processes of developing reading and writing skills.

In their research, Ms. Powell, Aaron, and the other students came across resources on the media about social justice. The Parkland shooting was still very much on their minds, and youth leadership was at the forefront of many media stories nationally. But at the same time, state standards and skills still needed to be covered. Because students are more motivated to participate in activities that are culturally and socially relevant to themselves, incorporating critical media literacy into academic subjects can increase motivation and engagement in core academic content (Morrell et al., 2013). Aaron, along with two of his classmates, Ms. Powell, and Ms. Edwards, co-created a Monday through Friday routine that centered around a high-interest topic, such a school shooting or in-school segregation. But they also embedded in their routine standards and skills that would be met and practiced each day. They decided that the class would vote on a topic on each Friday and that Ms. Powell would teach necessary standards and skills throughout the following week using materials, both print and media, centered around their agreed-upon topic. Vocabulary, morphology, sentence and paragraph structures and cohesion, mechanics such as punctuation, spelling, genre, themes, annotations, citations, summarization, reasoning and integration, critical analyses, and other knowledge and skills of print conventions would be taught using multiple sources of literacies, including news articles, op-eds, memes, poetry, or paragraphs from books.

It was also important to Aaron to promote intergenerational interaction around literacies, for both younger people like his siblings and cousins, and older people like his parents, teachers, and pastor. There remains in our culture a pervasive and powerful belief that literacy can transform individuals in ways that touch virtually all aspects of their lives (Williams, 2017). Aaron knew that reading and writing could lead to getting a better education, landing a good job, being a better citizen, and achieving better personal economics. But he wanted to showcase literacies outside of academic literacy. Therefore, Ms. Powell began the process of immersing herself in literacy communities far away from the formal institutions of learning: places where writers, poets, and thinkers on the periphery of English classrooms did their work (Winn, 2013).

The district coordinator invited Ms. Powell to various events such as a poetry slam, a film festival, and a music production at a local teen zone. Aaron requested that other pieces of "outside" literacies artifacts, such as those from the teen zone, churches, or individual homes, be brought into English classrooms and shared with his peers as well. He wanted the teachers at the school to see the full spectrum of authoring and coauthoring already existing in their communities, including the children's books he read to his siblings and cousins, old letters one of his cousins found in an attic, and a rap song that his best friend wrote.

Ms. Powell was pleasantly surprised at both the eager participation of her students and their higher assessment scores. After Ms. Powell and her students agreed on incorporating daily independent reading, all of her students were reading and writing more proficiently and fluently, and not only in her class. Other teachers noticed a significant improvement in the students' skills and engagement. Aaron, however, was not surprised. And he was thrilled to see the change he had wanted for himself and his peers. Through this collaboration, Ms. Powell had more knowledge and power to urge the school to move toward an inclusive literacy curriculum in which a separate literacy special and intervention education class no longer would be needed for readers perceived as "below grade level." Moving from response, restoration, and repair to leadership and collaboration in literacies, both in and out of educational institutions, brings about sustainability among all generations who embrace and practice multiple literacies. In developing collaborative literacies, voice and behaviors are seen as forms of positive agency that can be developed into action. In addition, collaboration and a shift in sharing power, in turn, allow for all voices to be heard. A flexible definition of leadership, while envisioning multiple paths to leadership, allows opportunities for people of all ages to lead for change and growth in myriads of ways. Only then can leadership and sustainability lead to a strong sense of identities in literacies.

CHAPTER 9

Recognizing Literacies and Identities

Jayden was publicly accused of plagiarism. He had transferred from a pre-dominantly Black school in a low-income area of a city to a predominantly White school in a higher-income neighborhood. Even though he was in 10th grade, Jayden had not learned about references and citations at his old school. He had never done a research project, or much writing, for that matter. Most of his literacy education had involved worksheets and out-dated books. The fact that Jayden devoured even the outdated books was what made everyone, from Jayden's teachers to his parents, declare Jayden as "smart." However, the dilapidated schools Jayden had attended had leak-ing roofs, warped floors, broken windows, lack of heat, nonworking toilets, class sizes of 45 to 50 students, significant teacher turnover and shortages, and lack of books, computers, and other literacy artifacts.

Jayden's aunt told him he was lucky to be in his new neighborhood and new school. But Jayden said he didn't feel lucky. He had lost his father to gun violence when he was in elementary school and more recently he had lost his mother to an opioid overdose. Not only had he experienced significant personal losses, but he was experiencing culture shock at being moved to a new school, one that seemed to him to be a sea of White. Jayden's new world was bewildering to him. Jayden thought he was smart. He had an insatiable curiosity, learned to read quickly in kindergarten, and enjoyed reading as much as he could over his school years. When Jayden was a young child, his father had told him he was smart and to never forget that. His mother told him he was smart almost daily until she died. And his aunt too, who recently took custody of him, told him he was smart and surely would make it in his new school. But upon confronting the reality of being at his new school, he told his uncle that he felt that he was the stupidest person in the entire place.

As graded papers were being returned to students, Jayden's teacher called Jayden to his desk, admonishing Jayden for not properly citing works. Jayden listened politely but soon realized the entire class was quiet and lis-tening too. Seeing that he was being called out for plagiarism in his English class, Jayden quickly surmised that the ownership of literature and literacy belonged to White people. Understandably, after carrying a difficult nar-rative in his life, Jayden's grief and anger were triggered. He stood up and stammered that he had enough of White people books, White people words, and White people ways. It didn't help that one of his classmates piped up that there were even authoritative white papers, such as government reports or business marketing documents. Another classmate quipped that was why paper itself was white too. Jayden didn't stick around to hear the rest of the commentaries from his classmates. He stormed out and walked to the safety of his new home.

Jayden had enough talent but not the academic grade-point average to play on the basketball team. But his aunt and uncle wanted Jayden to see possibilities in an academic or business environment, so they started to take steps to secure support for Jayden at his new school. While a referral for special education was not in their plans, Jayden's aunt and uncle were told that special education was the only way Jayden could get extra help in his new school. The psychologist and social worker had reviewed Jayden's huge folder of accumulated records from seven different schools. At an initial team meeting, the folder happened to be placed on the table in front of Jayden. While the team members were discussing Jayden's life and schooling, Jayden quietly stared at the folder, being polite and in the throes of deep grief and bewilderment. The psychologist suddenly tapped on the folder and called Jayden by name. She pointed out that both his 3rd- and 4th-grade test scores were in the 80th to 90th percentiles. Jayden whispered that he had no idea what that meant. The psychologist explained that it meant Jayden was very smart, but then she asked, What happened? Why did his test scores consistently drop until he arrived in 10th grade at the new school? At that point, Jayden's uncle stood up, declaring the meeting over, and asserted that the circumstances of Jayden's school history were out of Jayden's control.

Jayden's uncle took Jayden by the elbow and they left the meeting together. But Jayden needed to pick up his backpack and books from the library before they left for home. Ms. Connor, the school's librarian, noticed the discontent on their faces. Even though she had not yet formally met Jayden, she knew who he was. She had heard through the student grapevine that Jayden was called out for plagiarism and that he remarked about everything being White. She also heard through the staff grapevine that Jayden was a student who should be referred for special education. After seeing Jayden and his uncle leave the meeting room and cut through the library and out the door, Ms. Connor decided that restorative literacies were especially needed for Jayden, whom she knew as a smart student who regularly checked out books and was one of the most frequent library patrons at the school.

UNCOVERING IDENTITIES

Ms. Connor saw that Jayden was starting to disengage himself as he confronted grief and the entire White system, which he felt was too bewildering to overcome. But Ms. Connor wasn't sure how to help Jayden reconcile the differences between his White classmates and himself, and the striking socioeconomic differences between his old school and his new one. At the same time, while Ms. Connor was working toward equity and inclusion in her library and school, she didn't want to put Jayden in a vulnerable place of authority on his race. But most of all, she wanted to support Jayden as he adjusted to his new environment, without singling him out.

There is danger in the single story. Single stories only tell part of a story, not the entire story with all its richness, layers, and complexity. "The single story creates stereotypes. And the problem with stereotypes is not that they are untrue, but that they are incomplete. They make one story become the only story" (Adichie, 2009). Looking through the small pile of library books Jayden inadvertently had left behind in his rush to leave the school, Ms. Connor was surprised to see books about octopuses, narwhals, seahorses, starfish, and other creatures of the sea. Was he hoping to be a marine biologist someday? Here was a complex story. Not only did Jayden's choice of books challenge Ms. Connor's preconceived notions about Jayden based on his personal history, his socioeconomic status, and his race, but she caught herself and was humbled by her own surprise.

The discovery of the books Jayden left behind was an opportunity for Ms. Connor to finally meet and begin a conversation with Jayden. It turned out that Jayden had found a photograph of his father in the process of moving out of his old home. In that photograph, Jayden's father was proudly holding up an eel-like fish with a long spotted body and a slender beak-like snout. Jayden did not know what kind of a fish it was, and he wasn't sure where the picture was taken. Since he had discovered the wealth of resources in his new school library, he made it a personal mission, even though the process was a bit haphazard, to find out the kind of fish his father had caught.

Ms. Connor decided to invite students and staff visiting her library to bring a mystery photograph to research. One student brought a postcard and another decided to bring a handwritten note. She scanned and posted the artifacts on a bulletin board and began the process of helping her students and staff collaboratively look for clues and make discoveries about their mysteries. Slowly but surely, captions were appearing below each photograph, and people enthusiastically were returning to read the discoveries about each picture. Jayden learned that his father had caught a longnose gar and surmised that he might have caught it from the western basin of Lake Erie. Jayden, Ms. Connor, and other students and staff learned that even exotic-looking fish existed in their area of inland lakes and rivers, not just in oceans.

Not only did the students learn new information and how to source that information, but the artifacts in the library began a reflective move from stereotypes to stories of humanity for both students and staff. Single stories make "our recognition of equal humanity difficult" and emphasize "how we are different rather than how we are similar" (Adichie, 2009). Through this photo project, Jayden was beginning to become reengaged at school, and other students were beginning to get to know him. They learned about his memories of his family and his love for them. They learned that Jayden had enjoyed fishing with his father and that he had an innate sense of curiosity and caring about the world around him. Inviting artifacts from homes and communities that foster emerging stories was a small start toward restorative literacies for both Jayden and his peers.

DECENTERING WHITENESS

Jayden found himself overwhelmed by White people books, White people words, and White people ways, and even white paper. "Whiteness is everywhere at work; in the parks; on television; in films, books, magazines, newspapers; on university campuses; in the board rooms of corporations; in the laws, institutions, and systems; in everyday discourse and language; on the streets; at the banks, homeownerships, and the courthouses; in hiring and promotions; in attitudes and behavior; and in schools" (Pinder, 2015, p. 96). White-dominated educational contexts often are characterized by a curriculum that overrepresents White perspectives, and instruction that privileges White ways of knowing and being in the classroom, to the detriment of students of color (Borsheim-Black & Sarigianides, 2019). Pinder (2015) noted that the ontological positioning of Whiteness as an unmarked and unraced category, as a "normal" part of society, is terrifying to Blacks and other non-Whites.

Jayden, too, was terrified. When he found himself in trouble for seemingly plagiarizing one of his projects, Jayden was seen as abnormal or even criminal, not as a smart student who happened to have a huge knowledge gap in his educational background. Jayden thought he was honoring other people's quotes. He had had no prior opportunities to learn about the intricacies of quotation marks, dating, footnotes, or reference lists. In not acknowledging Jayden's complex story, his teacher and special education team were operating from a systemic sense of fairness in a color-blind manner by directing him to special education or even punishment. His teachers meant well. They thought that special education truly would be a resource and a source of support for Jayden. They thought they were doing the right thing by making sure that Jayden understood the consequences of plagiarism in high school rather than out in the real world, where the consequences are harsher. However, Jayden's teachers were not entirely culpable as individuals. The teachers' response to Jayden's plagiarism was a natural result of the built-in structure and system, but a structure and system that needed to be disrupted.

The identities of those sitting at tables of power in this country have remained remarkably similar: White, male, middle- and upper-class, and able-bodied (DiAngelo, 2018). DiAngelo notes that our sense of White fragility occurs when we consider a challenge to our racial worldviews as a challenge to our very identities as good, moral people, triggering a range of defensive responses such as argumentation, silence, and withdrawal from difficult situations. Jayden's educational team argued in various ways that the onus was on Jayden for his plagiarism and short outburst. They argued that race and poverty, which unfortunately are closely tied, had nothing to do with Jayden's predicament. The team made it clear that it was about Jayden being in 10th grade and that he should have known better about citing works. While our nation currently considers itself as color-blind and post-racial, difficult conversations about race continue in our schools, workplaces, and communities. "Denial is the heartbeat of racism" (Kendi, 2019, p. 9). The problem with being "not racist" is that it signifies neutralism, actually becoming a mask for racism and maintaining the status quo. The opposite of racism is *antiracism*, a concept where racism is identified, described, and dismantled (Kendi, 2019).

Jayden needed someone like Ms. Connor, who was White, to take him under her wing in an antiracist, not a patronizing, manner immediately after his "first strike" as a new student to the school. White teachers, not just people of color who have already suffered generations at the hands of white supremacy, must shoulder the work of antiracism in English classrooms (Tanner, 2019). Ms. Connor took it upon herself to tell the teaching staff and principal that as a librarian, she would make time to teach Jayden about citations and references. During a short period of bonding, Ms. Connor listened to and acknowledged Jayden's feelings of being criminalized and marginalized. However, throughout their lessons, she slowly brought back Jayden's sense of being smart by teaching him the conventions of academic scholarship. Jayden, who was not only smart but also had a gentle, caring personality, wanted to do right in all fronts of his life, and that included referencing other people's work.

In addition, Ms. Connor taught several sessions on sourcing, citing, and referencing to Jayden's entire class, but with decentering Whiteness in mind. She asked, "Whose story are we missing?" (Gyasi, 2016, p. 226). How do we see parallel and intersecting narratives, rather than dichotomous thought patterns, the flawed binaries of "those people" and "us"? (Kroll, 2008). Even though most students at Jayden's school were White, a majority-minority is emerging nationwide. Among the nation's newborns, babies who will be entering public schools in 4 or 5 years, we now have a non-White majority. In many regions, Whites will be part of a rapidly declining minority in a highly unequal society with no serious plan for equality and integration (Mordechay & Orfield, 2017). Learning in a racially diverse, integrated educational environment will have significant social and social–cognitive benefits for all students. Students in heterogeneous school environments learn to appreciate and respect racial differences, overcome racial stereotypes, avoid scapegoating, prevent racial hatreds and fears, and develop positive racial attitudes (Killen et al., 2007).

Decentering Whiteness across the board was needed at Jayden's school, especially after Jayden pointed out to his peers the Whiteness of their environment. When students of color see their identity, their histories, and their epistemologies centered in their education, they learn more and can better demonstrate their learning in both traditional and nontraditional measures of learning (Utt, 2018). Ms. Connor slowly had been adding books about characters of color and books written by authors of color to her library collection. But these books seldom were checked out, even as she publicly displayed them along with a short personal recommendation. Ms. Connor realized that her student population was in a place of thinking that race and diversity were issues belonging to "other" people and not themselves. She couldn't blame the students or the educators. Curricular standards and textbooks in schools establish and normalize White/Western ways of knowing. Such standards and textbooks valorize White/Western people as the heroes of democracy, philosophy, science, and art. By doing so, they partially or wholly erase non-White/Western philosophies and contributions, while also sanitizing the White/Western colonial violence from which anti-colonial epistemologies were born (Utt, 2018). Yet if programs like ethnic studies are offered only to students of color, little change is demanded of White people, who benefit from current systems of oppression. Educational approaches for White students also need to decenter Whiteness and offer truths about its inherent oppressiveness (Utt, 2018).

Contemporary art and culture, in literary, musical, and visual spheres, can vividly yoke together the racial realities that typically have been kept separate. With an emphasis on shared and interconnected history and experiences, students can learn to read and see "double" by looking for evidence of White-centered material and seeking parallel narratives beyond the dominant cultural scripts (Kroll, 2008).

Knowing that she couldn't jump right into the issue of racism and White privilege, Ms. Connor started by teaching her students how to grapple with "fake news." While we are not yet in post-racial times, our society may be in a post-information age. In a post-information age, people need to create meaning through a nonlinear, interactive, and participatory social network, one that juxtaposes multi-intelligences, multiliteracies, and multilanguages, and is multimodal. It is no longer enough to just look things up on search engines and cite and reference the information. A metaliterate learner, having metacognitive, cognitive, affective, and behavioral awareness, can become a researcher, participant, communicator, translator, author, teacher, collaborator, producer, and publisher (Mackey & Jacobson, 2011).

In taking steps toward developing metaliteracy in her students, Ms. Connor allowed her students to choose a social justice topic to research. It did not necessarily have to be a topic that they liked, but it had to be a topic that ticked them off or that they felt involved some sort of injustice. They could work in teams, in pairs, or individually. While some students chose topics such as gun violence, mass shootings, or police brutality, others chose to focus on the safety and liability of autonomous vehicles, lack of fresh vegetables and fruit in urban areas, and whether all countries should have open borders. Jayden chose to explore the topic of student-athlete eligibility and whether the requirements kept athletes eligible to compete at the expense of their education. This was a topic that Jayden understood on a personal level. He was told that he could take "easy" classes, such as physical education and independent reading, to bring up his grades in order to play on the basketball team. But his uncle had pushed Jayden to take more rigorous academic classes that would better his chances for college and future economic success.

After the students picked their topics, Ms. Connor projected a media bias chart (Ad Fontes Media, 2020) on her whiteboard with a number of logos of websites and news organizations, including HuffPost, BuzzFeed, CNN, NPR, *Time*, *The Wall Street Journal*, and Fox News. The chart placed the logos from top to bottom in a range from factual and original reporting to propaganda and fabricated information. The chart also showed placements of the logos in a range from left to right as skewing from most extreme or hyperpartisan liberal to neutral to extreme or hyperpartisan conservative. Ms. Connor asked her students to seek five articles from news sources that had reported on their topic. However, the articles were to be chosen from sources in the neutral area as well as from both the left and right extremes of the chart. The students were to briefly summarize each of their articles in a sentence or two and place their summarization on an outline of their own copy of the media bias chart.

During a restorative circle, Ms. Connor asked her students to think about other perspectives in reviewing the range of sources in their charts. Her position on antiracism moved from simple inclusion of diverse books in her library to teaching students how to read differently, engaging White readers in reflecting on ways Whiteness influences personal responses to texts (Borsheim-Black & Sarigianides, 2019). How might a person of color feel? Where do their families' belief systems fit into their responses? What would a person with a disability think? How does social media work to narrow perspectives through algorithms and echo chambers? And how can opportunities for stories and re-storying be made? While these were courageous, and even controversial, questions, the point was not to use knowledge or rhetoric toward advancing an argument, but to apply critical thinking, decenter and de-normalize Whiteness, deepen understanding, and build empathy (Kroll, 2008; Noddings & Brooks, 2016).

TOXIC POSITIVITY

American public education currently is facing the realities that our teacher force is mostly White, that the student population is highly diverse and will continue to become more diverse, and that race-based disparities continue to exist in almost every dimension of educational systems. Diversity is not a choice, but our responses to it certainly are (G. R. Howard, 2016). As long as Whiteness continues to be the norm, post-Whiteness is impossible (Pinder, 2015). Instead, educators can learn to see White as a race and culture itself, while recognizing the deeply entrenched, normalized, privileged, and institutional impact on the culture, linguistics, economics, politics, and abilities of other population groups. Any attempt to escape, avoid, quash, or silence negative emotions or experiences is an unwillingness to stare down life's most terrifying and difficult challenges and take action (Manson, 2016). Toxic positivity is a belief that if a person stays positive, looks on the bright side, or is happy, then that person can overcome any obstacle. Toxic positivity results in people belittling, ignoring, and alienating the challenges of life rather than validating and supporting their feelings and difficult experiences.

Unfortunately, toxic positivity is a veiled form of meritocracy. The "traditional view of meritocracy holds that most inequalities are not created by some central authority or discriminatory policy but arise out of the individual's innate or acquired skills, capabilities, education, and other resources" (Ornstein, 2007, p. 171). Jayden persistently was told he was smart. Of course, Jayden is smart. But success in schools involves much more than just having an optimal set of characteristic traits, such as smartness, grit, perseverance, passion, resiliency, or optimism. Unfortunately, White people generally are allowed to have problems, and they've historically been granted the power to define and respond to them, but people of color regularly are viewed and treated as the problem (Alexander, 2020). After all, Jayden demonstrated all of the above-mentioned traits when he stood up in his class and pointed out the Whiteness around him, and when, along with his uncle, he left the difficult conditions in the meeting, making it clear that they would not tolerate the kinds of disparagement that were being directed against them. But when such characteristics are applied in seemingly non-normative ways in school environments, the behavior too often is seen as negative, and the person, like Jayden, as the problem.

How a person is storied by other people—whether through gossip, prejudice, ignorance, or all three—has a direct effect on the range of social, professional, and economic options that are open to that person (Randall, 2014). Schools should not be in the business of deciding appropriate character traits or of changing personalities, nor should students be required to check their identities at the doors. Certainly, there must be a level of decorum for an environment that is conducive to learning, but simply faulting

Jayden for plagiarism, an unknown concept to him, was more likely to, and did, anger Jayden. Acknowledging the feelings of users of literacies is of pivotal importance to the larger social and educational project of humanizing literacy learning. Language and literacy are among the most humane of all practices; speaking, writing, reading, and imaging are the ways we tell human stories, forge relationships, and make sense of identities as humans (Leander & Ehret, 2019).

FOSTERING READERS' IDENTITIES

Antiracism is a big wheel to turn in our society. But Jayden needed to feel immediately valued and treated with dignity at this pivotal point in his educational career. When Jayden had the opportunity, he was an engaged reader, even during his difficult childhood. Engagement in literacies is the emotional involvement and absorption of the reader in the process of responding to the content of reading (Harris & Hodges, 1995). However, Jayden was in danger of losing his sense of engagement in his new school as he began to consider the ownership of literacies as belonging to academia or to White people. In turn, Jayden was in danger of being marginalized as a result of rigid forms of punishment for plagiarism or of unwarranted placement in special education.

Continually developing a set of practices in literacies over a lifespan entails motivation and engagement (Frankel et al., 2016), but practices in literacies also should consider readers' identities. Identity grows out of a distinction between one's true inner self and an outer world of social rules and norms that does not adequately recognize that inner self's worth or dignity (Fukuyama, 2018). In other words, all people, including Jayden, have found themselves at odds with their larger community. In the same vein, reading identities can be understood in terms of how capable individuals believe they are in comprehending texts, the value they place on reading, and their understandings of what it means to be a particular type of reader within a given context (Hall, 2016). Even though Jayden originally considered himself to be a good reader and knew that reading and writing were important for educational and economic success, he began to doubt his identity as a literate being when he got in trouble for plagiarizing.

According to Hall (2016), students in a year-long study who were seen as "poor readers" believed that even though they wanted to improve their reading, they, themselves, did not play a role in or have control over their reading development (Hall, 2016). These "poor readers" determined that it was the teachers—with the systemic and structural power—who should be able to shape them into good readers. Our culture retains a pervasive and powerful belief that literacy is transformative to education, employment, and social standing, but that transformation remains enmeshed in institutions and scholarship. When people are seen reading and writing, are their identities shaping their literacy practices, or are their literacy practices helping to construct their identities? Both are happening. In restorative literacies, educators are mindful of the intersections between literacy practices and issues of identity (Williams, 2017).

Identity and engagement as readers, writers, and literate beings come into play when cognition, metacognition, text complexity, authorship, race, culture, linguistics, economics, politics, abilities, background knowledge, purposes, motivation, agency, inclusion, and relationships are noticed, heard, embraced, and empowered. Even though all the terms listed in the previous sentence are loaded with multiple and weighty meanings, educators cultivating restorative literacies move beyond the "basic skills" of reading and writing in order to respond to, restore, repair, and reconcile the relationship between the backgrounds and perspectives, as well as the variable skills, proficiencies, and fluencies, of readers; the multiple texts readers encounter; and the authors of such texts.

Restorative Literacies and Restorative Care

Schools are not always safe places. In our current climate of standardized testing, worry over children having dyslexia or learning disabilities, and a deficit-based model of education, there is little room for children to be delightfully messy. Too often, mistakes, miscues, and errors in reading and writing are duly noticed, counted, and corrected, instead of being viewed as a natural—and messy—part of learning about multiple literacies (Wolter, 2018). Students need plenty of safe harbors where they can stumble, play, practice, and learn far away from teachers' pens of any color (M. Johnson, 2020). Not only does educational policy fail our children, but schools themselves are no longer physically safe. Our lives literally may depend on treating education as our greatest collective responsibility (Kundu, 2020). All elements of restorative literacies can bring back a sense of collectiveness, community peace, and an ability to pursue a wide range of literacies.

The future science(s) of reading cannot be limited to a single perspective drawn from the findings of a largely White, Western view of neurology, development, and pedagogy. They cannot be limited to discrete levels of language (orthography, phonology, and semantics) without accounting for the reciprocal relations between other dimensions of language-in-use: discourse, pragmatics, rhetoric, and the culture it maintains and conveys (Gabriel, 2020). Instead, the elements of restorative literacies can position student and educator choice, voice, and engagement as a way of remaking, reimagining, and re-mediating education for everyone. And instead of attempting to "empower" students, educators can cultivate the genius, brilliance, intellect, ability, cleverness, and artistry that already lie within students (Muhammad, 2020).

Restorative literacies serve as a medium for restorative care toward establishing peace in both schools and communities. After all, literacies *are* about building connections and strengthening relationships. The cultural, linguistic, economic, political, and dis/ableist views, backgrounds, and perspectives of all people are validated. The variable skills, proficiencies, and fluencies of readers, and effectiveness of writers, have multiple ways to grow in an intentional system of response, repair, and restoration in an educational setting. Noticing the language of stories, compassionate listening, expanding the concept of literacy and what it means to be literate, restoring relationships, repairing harm, strengthening agency, developing leadership and sustainability, and, most of all, recognizing literacies and identities are essential steps toward restorative literacies.

All elements—noticing, listening, expanding, restoring, repairing, strengthening, developing, and recognizing—of restorative literacies are disruptive to the disparaging status quo of our educational systems and structures. Utilizing each or all of these elements supports efforts toward antiracism and anti-ableism. Both educators and students together are nudged toward seeking visionary ways, even if seemingly uncomfortable or troublesome for some people, to change or navigate how schools are run and how students develop and strengthen multiple literacies.

All of the elements of restorative literacies bring about humility, humanity, and authenticity, not only in educators, but also in administrators, policymakers, community members, students, and families. Changing outcomes for a student, a classroom, a school, or a district cannot be done without changing one's own behavior and thinking. Sometimes educators fail or undermine their own work, but they can forgive themselves and continue moving forward (Minor, 2019). The ways that schools traditionally teach reading and writing per se, ways that are not working, must be abandoned. Through an intentional system of response, repair, and restoration in an educational or virtual setting, restorative literacies can build and strengthen positive relationships between the backgrounds and perspectives, as well as the variable skills, proficiencies, and fluencies, of readers, the multiple texts readers encounter, and the authors of such texts. In other words, restorative literacies embrace a sense of humanity to the multiple forms of languages, linguistics, and literacies that children bring to schools.

STORIES OF HUMANITY

Fully hearing and responding to stories about identities and literacies is a crucial first step toward improving reading and writing skills. Randall (2014) asked: "What issues do we bring to the surface about our development as persons, about our relationships, about our self-consciousness itself, when we extend it to include the possibility that we are each in the midst of our own unfolding novel, as its author/narrator, its protagonist, and its reader all at once?" (p. 19). Students bring stories of humanity to schools.

How did the students whom we've been following do after experiencing the restorative literacies approach? After Alec's mother died and he wanted to read like Ellie, the relationships that educators built with Alec and his father paved a positive way for Alec's three younger brothers in the school. And Alec became an enthusiastic reader to the point where his father often had to remind him to put his book down and mow the lawn. Olivia, once the subject of a series of contentious IEP meetings, arrived at middle school with very little need for special education. While many adolescents go through a period of angst, Olivia joined book clubs, made friends, and thrived. Diego, who was juggling multiple languages, did not "test well" until later in his school career. But he continued to happily explore and grow in both his own literacies and school-like literacy. With Ms. Evans's advocacy, Diego's subsequent teachers began to put more weight on their observations and expertise than on simple test scores. Lamar, who waited to complete his schoolwork until it was sent home where he could get help, and Trevor, who diligently complied by copying his schoolwork, both became agents in their literacies through a workshop model. Lamar and Trevor moved from a sense of passivity to being fully engaged and active learners. And they made growth by leaps and bounds in their reading and writing skills. Both Aaron and Jayden grew to be strong readers and leaders in their school and community. Aaron, outspoken by nature, was on the forefront of social issues, and Jayden, in his introverted way, wrote and published about a range of social justice topics for both the school's website and the local teen zone. Aaron graduated and went on to college, where he majored in education and social work. Jayden needed one more year of credits before graduating, but he was well on his way.

Educators like Mr. Delaney, Ms. Evans, Ms. Morgan, Ms. Walker, Ms. Kate, Ms. Powell, and Ms. Connor not only needed to hear the stories of their students, but also learned to listen to their inner voices and to share stories themselves. Even though educators hold the power in school systems, they too are vulnerable and open to building relationships with students, families, and colleagues. With restorative literacies, students and educators constantly question who has caused harm and who has experienced harm. When stories unfold but are untold, they may become convoluted, preventing students, those without power, from thriving.

Restoration of health, strength, and well-being often is seen as an escape or a healing space away from the busyness and stress of the outside world, but restoration of relationships between readers and writers, and listeners and speakers, can be woven throughout people's daily lives, in schools and in communities. While restorative practice can transform relationships in criminal justice, social work, counseling, organizational management, and education, literacies and restorative literacies are intertwined in every aspect of our modern lives. In schools, taking a restorative literacies approach to teaching reading and writing skills and processes can make a world of difference, not only for disfranchised students, but for *all* students. Caring, relational teaching often involves learning a different model than what educators are taught. Even though relationships are not easy, focusing on teaching without relationships makes the job harder, and in some instances close to impossible (J. R. Howard et al., 2020). Restorative literacies acknowledge and foster cultural, linguistic, economic, political, and dis/ableist views of literacies. When the voices of both students and educators are brought to the forefront, authenticity and validation of literacies can permeate teaching and learning in a reciprocal and mutual manner. And restorative literacies can bring about the important conversations needed to embrace and sustain diversity in a global society.

References

Ad Fontes Media. (2020). *Media bias chart.* https://www.adfontesmedia.com/?v=402f03a963ba

Adichie, C. N. (2009). *The danger of a single story.* TED. https://www.ted.com/talks/chimamanda_ngozi_adichie_the_danger_of_a_single_story?language=en

Afflerbach, P., & Harrison, C. (2017). What is engagement, how is it different from motivation, and how can I promote it? *Journal of Adolescent & Adult Literacy, 61*(2), 217–220.

Alexander, M. (2020, January 17). The injustice of this moment is not an "aberration." *The New York Times.* https://www.nytimes.com/2020/01/17/opinion/sunday/michelle-alexander-new-jim-crow.html

Allington, R. (2013). What really matters when working with struggling readers. *The Reading Teacher, 66*(7), 520–530.

Allington, R. L., & McGill-Franzen, A. (2010). Why so much oral reading? In E. H. Hiebert & D. R. Reutzel (Eds.), *Revisiting silent reading: New directions for teachers and researchers* (pp. 45–56). International Reading Association.

American Library Association. (2019, June 25). *Access to library resources and services for minors: An interpretation of the library bill of rights.* http://www.ala.org/advocacy/intfreedom/librarybill/interpretations/minors

Atwell, N. (2015). *In the middle: A lifetime of learning about writing, reading, and adolescents.* Heinemann.

Barton, D. (2017). *Literacy: An introduction to the ecology of written language.* Wiley.

Beers, G. K., & Probst, R. E. (2017). *Disrupting thinking: Why how we read matters.* Scholastic.

Bishop, R. S. (1990). Mirrors, windows, and sliding glass doors. *Perspectives, 6*(3), ix–xi.

Bizumic, B. (2019). *Ethnocentrism: Integrated perspectives.* Routledge.

Bolton, K. (2019). *Restorative practices: A science of human dignity.* Building a New Reality. https://www.buildinganewreality.com/restorative-practices-a-science-of-human-dignity/

Borsheim-Black, C., & Sarigianides, S. T. (2019). *Letting go of literary whiteness: Antiracist literature instruction for white students.* Teachers College Press.

Bouffard, J., Cooper, M., & Bergseth, K. (2017). The effectiveness of various restorative justice interventions on recidivism outcomes among juvenile offenders. *Youth Violence and Juvenile Justice, 15*(4), 465–480.

Boyes-Watson, C. (2005). Community is not a place but a relationship: Lessons for organizational development. *Public Organization Review, 5*(4), 359–374.

Brown, B. (2015). *Daring greatly: How the courage to be vulnerable transforms the way we live, love, parent, and lead.* Penguin.

Brownell, J. (2015). *Listening: Attitudes, principles, and skills.* Routledge.

Cain, S. (2013). *Quiet: The power of introverts in a world that can't stop talking.* Broadway Books.

Carey, R. L., Farinde-Wu, A., Milner, H. R. IV, & Delale-O'Connor, L. (2018). The culture and teaching gap: What is it, and how can teacher educators help to close it? In G. E. Hall, L. F. Quinn, & D. M. Gollnick (Eds.), *The Wiley handbook of teaching and learning* (pp. 59–78). Wiley.

Cartwright, K. B., & Duke, N. K. (2019). The DRIVE model of reading: Making the complexity of reading accessible. *The Reading Teacher, 73*(1), 7–15.

Centers for Disease Control. (2020, April 3). *Preventing adverse childhood experiences.* https://www.cdc.gov/violenceprevention/acestudy/fastfact.html

Clay, M. M. (1993). *Reading recovery: A guidebook for teachers in training.* Heinemann.

Clear, J. (2019). *Why facts don't change our minds.* https://jamesclear.com/why-facts-dont-change-minds

Conley, M. (2018). Building equity, literacy, and resilience within educational systems. In A. M. Lazar & P. R. Schmidt (Eds.), *Schools of promise for multilingual students: Transforming literacies, learning, and lives* (pp. 167–176). Teachers College Press.

Cook-Sather, A. (2020). Student voice across contexts: Fostering student agency in today's schools. *Theory Into Practice, 59*(2), 182–191.

Cooperative Children's Book Center. (2020). *Publishing statistics on children's/YA books about people of color and First/Native Nations and by people of color and First/Native Nations authors and illustrators.* https://ccbc.education.wisc.edu/literature-resources/ccbc-diversity-statistics/diversity-statistics-faqs/

Copeland, M. (2005). *Socratic circles: Fostering critical and creative thinking in middle and high school.* Stenhouse.

Cornwall, G. (2017). *Jabari jumps.* Candlewick.

Costello, B., Wachtel, J., & Wachtel, T. (2019a). *Restorative circles in schools: Building community and enhancing learning.* International Institute for Restorative Practices.

Costello, B., Wachtel, J., & Wachtel, T. (2019b). *The restorative practices handbook: For teachers, disciplinarians and administrators.* International Institute for Restorative Practices.

Coulmas, F. (2013). *Sociolinguistics: The study of speakers' choices.* Cambridge University Press.

Craig, G. (2003). Children's participation through community development: Assessing the lessons from international experience. In C. Hallett & A. Prout (Eds.), *Hearing the voices of children* (pp. 54–72). Routledge.

Cramer, E., Little, M. E., & McHatton, P. A. (2018). Equity, equality, and standardization: Expanding the conversations. *Education and Urban Society, 50*(5), 483–501.

Crystal, D. (2003). *English as a global language.* Cambridge University Press.

Crystal, D. (2008). *Txtng: The gr8 db8.* Oxford University Press.

Crystal, D. (2010). *The Cambridge encyclopedia of language* (3rd ed.). Cambridge University Press.

DeFaveri, A. (2005). Breaking barriers: Libraries and socially excluded communities. *Information for Social Change, 21,* 27–34.

Denton, P. (2013). *The power of our words: Teacher language that helps children learn*. Center for Responsive Schools.

Derman-Sparks, L., & Edwards, J. O. (2010). *Anti-bias education for young children and ourselves*. National Association for the Education of Young Children.

DiAngelo, R. (2011). White fragility. *International Journal of Critical Pedagogy, 3*(3), 54–70.

DiAngelo, R. J. (2018). *White fragility: Why it's so hard for white people to talk about racism*. Beacon Press.

Dodell-Feder, D., & Tamir, D. I. (2018). Fiction reading has a small positive impact on social cognition: A meta-analysis. *Journal of Experimental Psychology: General, 147*(11), 1713–1727.

Dudley-Marling, C., & Lucas, K. (2009). Pathologizing the language and culture of poor children. *Language Arts, 86*(5), 362–370.

Dupree, C. H., & Fiske, S. T. (2019). Self-presentation in interracial settings: The competence downshift by white liberals. *Journal of Personality and Social Psychology, 117*(3), 579–604.

Dutro, E. (2019). *The vulnerable heart of literacy: Centering trauma as powerful pedagogy*. Teachers College Press.

Eck, D. (2006). *What is pluralism?* The Pluralism Project. Harvard University. https://pluralism.org/about

Everett, D. (2017). *How language began: The story of humanity's greatest invention*. Profile Books.

Farrall, M. L. (2012). *Reading assessment: Linking language, literacy, and cognition*. Wiley.

Ferdman, B. (1990). Literacy and cultural identity. *Harvard Educational Review, 60*(2), 181–204.

Ferri, B. A., & Connor, D. J. (2005). Tools of exclusion: Race, disability, and (re)segregated education. *Teachers College Record, 107*(3), 453–474.

Fisher, D., Frey, N., & Hattie, J. (2016). *Visible learning for literacy*. Corwin.

Fisher, D., Frey, N., & Lapp, D. (2012). *Text complexity: Raising rigor in reading*. International Reading Association.

Fisher, D., & Ivey, G. (2007). Farewell to *A Farewell to Arms*: Deemphasizing the whole-class novel. *Phi Delta Kappan, 88*(7), 494–497.

Fleischer, C., & Andrew-Vaughan, S. (2009). *Writing outside your comfort zone: Helping students navigate unfamiliar genres*. Heinemann.

Fleischman, S. (1986). *The whipping boy*. Greenwillow Books.

Fountas, I. C., & Pinnell, G. S. (1996). *Guided reading: Good first teaching for all children*. Heinemann.

Fountas, I. C., & Pinnell, G. S. (2018). Every child, every classroom, every day: From vision to action in literacy learning. *The Reading Teacher, 72*(1), 7–19.

Fox, D. L., Flynn, L., & Austin, P. (2015). Child leadership: Teachers' perceptions and influences. *Childhood Education, 91*(3), 163–168.

Fox, J. (2008). *Your child's strengths: Discover them, develop them, use them*. Penguin.

Fox, K. (2016). *Young voice, big impact*. National Association of Elementary School Principals. https://www.naesp.org/sites/default/files/Fox_ND16.pdf

Frankel, K. K., Becker, B. L., Rowe, M. W., & Pearson, P. D. (2016). From "what is reading?" to what is literacy? *Journal of Education, 196*(3), 7–17.

Fukuyama, F. (2018). *Identity: Contemporary identity politics and the struggle for recognition*. Profile Books.

Fullam, J. (2015). "Listen then, or, rather, answer": Contemporary challenges to Socratic education. *Educational Theory, 65*(1), 53–71.

Gabriel, R. (2020). The future of the science of reading. *The Reading Teacher, 74*(1), 11–18.

Gaffney, C. (2019). When schools cause trauma. *Teaching Tolerance Magazine.* https://www.tolerance.org/magazine/summer-2019/when-schools-cause-trauma

Gallagher, K. (2009). *Readicide: How schools are killing reading and what you can do about it.* Stenhouse.

Gallagher, M. (2009). Data collection and analysis. In K. Tisdall, J. M. Davis, & M. Gallagher (Eds.), *Researching with children and young people: Research design, methods and analysis* (pp. 65–127). Sage.

Galletta, A., & Torre, M. E. (2019, August). Participatory action research in education. *Oxford research encyclopedia of education.* https://oxfordre.com/education /education/view/10.1093/acrefore/9780190264093.001.0001/acrefore -9780190264093-e-557

Gardner, H. (2006). *Changing minds: The art and science of changing our own and other people's minds.* Harvard Business Review Press.

Garland-Thomson, R. (2016, August 21). Becoming disabled. *The New York Times.* https://www.nytimes.com/2016/08/21/opinion/sunday/becoming-disabled. html?searchResultPosition=1

Gelfand, M. (2018). *Rule makers, rule breakers: How tight and loose cultures wire our world.* Scribner.

Gerald, C. (2018, December 8). T.M. Landry and the tragedy of viral success stories. *The New York Times.* https://www.nytimes.com/2018/12/08/opinion/sunday/ tm-landry-louisiana-school-abuse.html

Gillies, R. M. (2014). Developments in classroom-based talk. *International Journal of Educational Research, 63*, 63–68.

Givens, J. R., & Suad Nasir, N. (2019). We dare say love: Black male student experiences and the possibilities therein. In H. Suad Nasir, J. R. Givens, & C. P. Chatmon (Eds.), *We dare say love: Supporting achievement in the educational lives of black boys* (pp. 1–12). Teachers College Press.

Gladwell, M. (2008). *Outliers: The story of success.* Little, Brown.

Gold, C. (2016). *The silenced child: From labels, medications, and quick-fix solutions to listening, growth, and lifelong resilience.* Da Capo Lifelong Books.

Gonzalez, T. E., Hernandez-Saca, D. I., & Artiles, A. J. (2017). In search of voice: Theory and methods in K-12 student voice research in the US, 1990–2010. *Educational Review, 69*(4), 451–473.

Goodley, D. (2014). *Dis/ability studies: Theorising disablism and ableism.* Routledge.

Gorski, P. C. (2016). Poverty and the ideological imperative: A call to unhook from deficit and grit ideology and to strive for structural ideology in teacher education. *Journal of Education for Teaching, 42*(4), 378–386.

Gratz, A. (2017). *Refugee.* Scholastic.

Gyasi, Y. (2016). *Homegoing: A novel.* Vintage Books.

Haberman, M. (1991). The pedagogy of poverty versus good teaching. *The Phi Delta Kappan, 73*(4), 290–294.

Haberman, M. (2010). 11 consequences of failing to address the "pedagogy of poverty." *Phi Delta Kappan, 92*(2), 45.

Hall, L. A. (2016). The role of identity in reading comprehension development. *Reading & Writing Quarterly, 32*(1), 56–80.

Harmon, J., Martinez, M., Juarez, L., Wood, K., Simmerson, L., & Terrazas, C. (2019). An investigation of middle school classroom libraries. *Reading Psychology*, pp. 1–29.

Harris, T., & Hodges, R. E. (1995). *The literacy dictionary*. International Reading Association.

Hart, B., & Risley, T. R. (2003). The early catastrophe: The 30 million word gap by age 3. *American Educator, 27*(1), 4–9.

Harvey, S., & Ward, A. (2017). *From striving to thriving: How to grow confident, capable readers*. Scholastic.

Hassan, H., Asad, S., & Hoshino, Y. (2016). Determinants of leadership style in big five personality dimensions. *Universal Journal of Management, 4*(4), 161–179.

Hehir, T. (2005). *New directions in special education: Eliminating ableism in policy and practice*. Harvard Education Press.

Henderson, B. (2011). *The blind advantage: How going blind made me a stronger principal and how including children with disabilities made our school better for everyone*. Harvard Education Press.

Herr, J. (2018). Preface. In T. Miranda & J. Herr (Eds.), *The value of academic discourse: Conversations that matter* (pp. ix–x). Rowman & Littlefield.

Hirsch, E. D. (2007). *The knowledge deficit: Closing the shocking education gap for American children*. Houghton Mifflin Harcourt.

Hirsch, E. D. (2019). *Why knowledge matters: Rescuing our children from failed educational theories*. Harvard Education Press.

Hodges, T. S., Wright, K. L., Roberts, K. L., Norman, R. R., & Coleman, J. (2019). Equity in access? The number of the books available in grade 1, 3 and 5 classroom libraries. *Learning Environments Research, 22*(3), 427–441.

Howard, G. R. (2016). *We can't teach what we don't know: White teachers, multiracial schools*. Teachers College Press.

Howard, J. R., Milner-McCall, T., & Howard, T. (2020). *No more teaching without positive relationships*. Heinemann.

Howard, M. (2009). *RTI from all sides: What every teacher needs to know*. Heinemann.

Howard, T. (2020). Know your students well. In J. R. Howard, T. Milner-McCall, & T. Howard, *No more teaching without positive relationships* (pp. 13–19). Heinemann.

Hudley, A. H. C., & Mallinson, C. (2015). *Understanding English language variation in U.S. schools*. Teachers College Press.

International Institute for Restorative Practices. (2018). *What is restorative practices?* https://www.iirp.edu/restorative-practices/what-is-restorative-practices

International Literacy Association. (2018). *The case for children's rights to read*. https://literacyworldwide.org/docs/default-source/resource-documents/the-case -for-childrens-rights-to-read.pdf

International Literacy Association & National Council of Teachers of English. (2019). *How to help a child choose a book*. Read Write Think. http://www. readwritethink.org/parent-afterschool-resources/tips-howtos/help-child-choose -book-30320.html

Israel, E. (2002). Examining multiple perspectives in literature. In J. Holden & J. S. Schmit (Eds.), *Inquiry and the literary text: Constructing discussions in the English classroom* (pp. 89–103). National Council of Teachers of English.

Johnson, A. (2019). *A walk in their kicks: Literacy, identity, and the schooling of young Black males*. Teachers College Press.

Johnson, E. J. (2015). Debunking the "language gap." *Journal for Multicultural Education, 9*(1), 42–50.

Johnson, M. (2018, September 20). *Why students brag about not doing work (and what we can do about it)*. https://matthewmjohnson.com/2018/09/20/why-students-brag-about-not-doing-work-and-what-we-can-do-about-it/

Johnson, M. (2020). *Flash feedback: Responding to student writing better and faster without burning out*. Corwin.

Kaczmarczyk, A., Allee-Herndon, K. A., & Roberts, S. K. (2019). Using literacy approaches to begin the conversation on racial illiteracy. *The Reading Teacher, 72*(4), 523–528.

Kay, M. R. (2018). *Not light, but fire: How to lead meaningful race conversations in the classroom*. Stenhouse.

Kendi, I. X. (2019). *How to be an antiracist*. One World/Ballantine.

Khalaf, B. K. (2018). Traditional and inquiry-based learning pedagogy: A systematic critical review. *International Journal of Instruction, 11*(4), 545–564.

Killen, M., Crystal, D. S., & Ruck, M. (2007). The social developmental benefits of intergroup contact among children and adolescents. In E. Frankenberg & G. Orfield (Eds.), *Lessons in integration: Realizing the promise of racial diversity in American schools* (pp. 31–56). University of Virginia Press.

King, M. (2018). *The good neighbor: The life and work of Fred Rogers*. Abrams Press.

Kirkland, D. E. (2013). *A search past silence*. Teachers College Press.

Kirkland, D. E. (2014). Urban literacy learning. In H. R. Milner IV & K. Lomotey (Eds.), *Handbook of urban education* (pp. 394–412). Routledge.

Kohn, A. (2018, October 27). Science confirms it: People are not pets. *The New York Times*. https://www.nytimes.com/2018/10/27/opinion/sunday/science-rewards-behavior.html

Kolbas, E. D. (2018). *Critical theory and the literary canon*. Routledge.

Kroll, C. (2008). Imagining ourselves into transcultural spaces: Decentering Whiteness in the classroom. *Counterpoints, 321,* 29–46.

Kundu, A. (2020). *The power of student agency: Looking beyond grit to close the opportunity gap*. Teachers College Press.

Lazar, A. M. (2018). Schools of promise for multilingual students. In A. M. Lazar & P. R. Schmidt (Eds.), *Schools of promise for multilingual students: Transforming literacies, learning, and lives* (pp. 3–15). Teachers College Press.

Lazar, A. M., Edwards, P. A., & McMillon, G. T. (2012). *Bridging literacy and equity: The essential guide to social equity teaching*. Teachers College Press.

Leander, K. M., & Ehret, C. (2019). *Affect in literacy learning and teaching: Pedagogies, politics and coming to know*. Routledge.

Lemov, D., Driggs, C., & Woolway, E. (2016). *Reading reconsidered: A practical guide to rigorous literacy instruction*. Wiley.

Lesesne, T. S. (2010). *Reading ladders: Leading students from where they are to where we'd like them to be*. Heinemann.

Leslie, I. (2014). *Curious: The desire to know and why your future depends on it*. Basic Books.

Lipp, J., & Johnson, C. (2019). *Phonemic awareness and phonics in Reading Recovery*. Reading Recovery. https://readingrecovery.org/wp-content/uploads/2019/05/Phonemic_Awareness_Phonics.pdf

Lippi-Green, R. (2012). *English with an accent: Language, ideology and discrimination in the United States*. Routledge.

Loewen, J. W. (2008). *Lies my teacher told me: Everything your American history textbook got wrong*. The New Press.

Losen, D. J., & Martinez, T. (2013). *Out of school and off track: The overuse of suspensions in American middle and high schools*. The Civil Rights Project.

Lunsford, A. (2013). *Our semi-literate youth? Not so fast*. https://ssw.stanford.edu/sites/g/files/sbiybj10266/f/OPED_Our_Semi-Literate_Youth.pdf

Mackey, T. P., & Jacobson, T. E. (2011). Reframing information literacy as a meta-literacy. *College & Research Libraries, 72*(1), 62–78.

Manson, M. (2016). *The subtle art of not giving a f*ck: A counterintuitive approach to living a good life*. Macmillan.

Marinak, B. A., & Gambrell, L. B. (2016). *No more reading for junk: Best practices for motivating readers*. Heinemann.

Marino, J., & Eisenberg, M. (2018). Beyond the research project: Inquiry every day and every way. *Knowledge Quest, 47*(2), 56–60.

Martinez, M. G., Yokota, J., & Temple, C. (2017). *Thinking and learning through children's literature*. Rowman & Littlefield.

Mason, J. (2002). *Researching your own practice: The discipline of noticing*. Routledge.

Matusov, E., von Duyke, K., & Kayumova, S. (2016). Mapping concepts of agency in educational contexts. *Integrative Psychological and Behavioral Science, 50*(3), 420–446.

May, S. (2014). Justifying educational language rights. *Review of Research in Education, 38*(1), 215–241.

Mayall, B. (2008). Conversations with children: Working with generational issues. In P. Christensen & J. A. James (Eds.), *Research with children* (pp. 125–140). Routledge.

McCluskey, G., Lloyd, G., Stead, J., Kane, J., Riddell, S., & Weedon, E. (2008). "I was dead restorative today": From restorative justice to restorative approaches in school. *Cambridge Journal of Education, 38*(2), 199–216.

McKool, S. S., & Gespass, S. (2009). Does Johnny's reading teacher love to read? How teachers' personal reading habits affect instructional practices. *Literacy Research and Instruction, 48*(3), 264–276.

McPhee, J. (2017). *Draft No. 4: On the writing process*. Farrar, Straus and Giroux.

McTigue, E. M., Washburn, E. K., & Liew, J. (2009). Academic resilience and reading: Building successful readers. *The Reading Teacher, 62*(5), 422–432.

Merga, M. K. (2016). "I don't know if she likes reading": Are teachers perceived to be keen readers, and how is this determined? *English in Education, 50*(3), 255–269.

Miller, D. (2010). *The book whisperer: Awakening the inner reader in every child*. John Wiley & Sons.

Milner, H. R. IV. (2010). *Start where you are, but don't stay there*. Harvard Education Press.

Milner, H. R. IV. (2015). *Rac(e)ing to class: Confronting poverty and race in schools and classrooms*. Harvard Education Press.

Milner, H. R. IV. (2018, November 14). *Achieving the goal of leading for equity: Six imperatives* [Paper presentation]. Responsive Teaching Institute, Washtenaw Intermediate School District, Ann Arbor, MI, United States.

Milner, H. R. IV. (2020). *Brown* lecture: Disrupting punitive practices and policies: Rac(e)ing back to teaching, teacher preparation, and *Brown*. *Educational Researcher, 49*(3), 147–160.

Milner, H. R. IV, Cunningham, H. B., Delale-O'Connor, L., & Kestenberg, E. G. (2018). *"These kids are out of control": Why we must reimagine "classroom management" for equity.* Corwin.

Minor, C. (2019). *We got this! Equity, access, and the quest to be who our students need us to be.* Heinemann.

Miranda, T., & Herr, J. (2018). *The value of academic discourse: Conversations that matter.* Rowman & Littlefield.

Mitchell, C., & Sackney, L. (2016). School improvement in high-capacity schools: Educational leadership and living-systems ontology. *Educational Management Administration & Leadership, 44*(5), 853–868.

Moore, R. A., & Seeger, V. N. (Eds.). (2009). *Building classroom reading communities: Retrospective miscue analysis and Socratic circles.* Corwin.

Mora, O. (2019). *Saturday.* Little, Brown and Company.

Mordechay, K., & Orfield, G. (2017). Demographic transformation in a policy vacuum: The changing face of U.S. metropolitan society and challenges for public schools. *The Educational Forum, 81*(2), 193–203.

Morrell, E. (2018, November 14). *Culturally responsive literacy teaching: Inspiring readers and writers in diverse K–12 classrooms.* Responsive Teaching Institute, Washtenaw Intermediate School District.

Morrell, E., Dueñas, R., Garcia, V., & Lopez, J. (2013). *Critical media pedagogy: Teaching for achievement in city schools.* Teachers College Press.

Muhammad, G. (2020). *Cultivating genius: An equity framework for culturally and historically responsive literacy.* Scholastic.

Mullarkey, L. S., Recchia, S. L., Lee, S. Y., Shin, M. S., & Lee, Y. J. (2005). Manipulative managers and devilish dictators: Teachers' perspectives on the dilemmas and challenges of classroom leadership. *Journal of Early Childhood Teacher Education, 25*(2), 123–129.

National Council of Teachers of English. (2007). *Adolescent literacy: A policy research brief.* https://cdn.ncte.org/nctefiles/resources/positions/chron0907researchbrief.pdf

National Council of Teachers of English. (2015). *Resolution on the need for diverse children's and young adult books.* http://www2.ncte.org/statement/diverse-books/print/

National Council of Teachers of English. (2018). *The students' right to read.* https://ncte.org/statement/righttoreadguideline/

National Council of Teachers of English. (2019). *Statement on independent reading.* https://ncte.org/statement/independent-reading/

Nel, P. (2017). *Was the cat in the hat black? The hidden racism of children's literature, and the need for diverse books.* Oxford University Press.

Neuman, S. B., & Celano, D. (2006). The knowledge gap: Implications of leveling the playing field for low-income and middle-income children. *Reading Research Quarterly, 41*(2), 176–201.

Neuman, S. B., & Moland, N. (2019). Book deserts: The consequences of income segregation on children's access to print. *Urban Education, 54*(1), 126–147.

NGA/CCSSO. (2010). *Common core state standards.* Author.

Noddings, N., & Brooks, L. (2016). *Teaching controversial issues: The case for critical thinking and moral commitment in the classroom.* Teachers College Press.

Noguera, P., Darling-Hammond, L., & Friedlaender, D. (2015). *Equal opportunity for deeper learning.* Jobs for the Future. https://files.eric.ed.gov/fulltext/ED560802.pdf

Oatley, K. (2016). Fiction: Simulation of social worlds. *Trends in Cognitive Sciences, 20*(8), 618–628.

Ornstein, A. (2007). *Class counts: Education, inequality, and the shrinking middle class.* Rowman & Littlefield.

Osher, D., Bear, G. G., Sprague, J. R., & Doyle, W. (2010). How can we improve school discipline? *Educational Researcher, 39*(1), 48–58.

Otheguy, R., García, O., & Reid, W. (2015). Clarifying translanguaging and deconstructing named languages: A perspective from linguistics. *Applied Linguistics Review, 6*(3), 281–307.

Paris, D. (2012). Culturally sustaining pedagogy: A needed change in stance, terminology, and practice. *Educational Researcher, 41*(3), 93–97.

Paul, R., & Elder, L. (2006). *Critical thinking: Learn the tools the best thinkers use.* Prentice Hall.

Peplow, D. (2016). *Talk about books: A study of reading groups.* Bloomsbury.

Pinder, S. O. (2015). *Colorblindness, post-raciality, and whiteness in the United States.* Springer.

Pinker, S. (2003). *The language instinct: How the mind creates language.* Penguin UK.

Plaut, V. C., Thomas, K. M., Hurd, K., & Romano, C. A. (2018). Do color blindness and multiculturalism remedy or foster discrimination and racism? *Current Directions in Psychological Science, 27*(3), 200–206.

Plumb, J. L., Bush, K. A., & Kersevich, S. E. (2016). Trauma-sensitive schools: An evidence-based approach. *School Social Work Journal, 40*(2), 37–60.

Prochnik, G. (2011). *In pursuit of silence: Listening for meaning in a world of noise.* Anchor.

Prout, A. (2003). Participation, policy and the changing conditions of childhood. In C. Hallett & A. Prout (Eds.), *Hearing the voices of children* (pp. 27–41). Routledge.

Ramsey, P. (2004). *Teaching and learning in a diverse world: Multicultural education for young children* (3rd ed.). Teachers College Press.

Randall, W. L. (2014). *The stories we are: An essay on self-creation.* University of Toronto Press.

Rigby, J. G., Woulfin, S. L., & März, V. (2016). Understanding how structure and agency influence education policy implementation and organizational change. *American Journal of Education, 122*(3), 295–302.

Riley, K. (2019). Agency and belonging: What transformative actions can schools take to help create a sense of place and belonging? *Educational and Child Psychology, 36*(4), 91–103.

Ringel, P. (2016, October 1). How banning books marginalizes children. *The Atlantic.* https://www.theatlantic.com/entertainment/archive/2016/10/how-banned-books-marginalize-children/502424/

Ripp, P. (2017). *Passionate readers: The art of reaching and engaging every child.* Routledge.

Rodriguez, V., & Fitzpatrick, M. (2014). *The teaching brain: An evolutionary trait at the heart of education.* The New Press.

Rosenberg, M. (2015). *Nonviolent communication: A language of life: Life-changing tools for healthy relationships.* Puddle Dancer Press.

Ross, L. (2019). *Speaking up without tearing down.* Teaching Tolerance. https://www.tolerance.org/magazine/spring-2019/speaking-up-without-tearing-down

Rowe, K. (2004). *The importance of teaching: Ensuring better schooling by building teacher capacities that maximize the quality of teaching and learning provision—implications of findings from the international and Australian evidence-based research.* Australian Council for Educational Research. https://research.acer.edu.au/cgi/viewcontent.cgi?article=1010&context=learning_processes

Schaefer, R. T. (2008). *Encyclopedia of race, ethnicity, and society* (Vol. 1). Sage.

Seemiller, C. (2018). A competency-based model for youth leadership development. *Journal of Leadership Education, 17*(1), 56–72.

Sensoy, Ö., & DiAngelo, R. (2017). *Is everyone really equal? An introduction to key concepts in social justice education.* Teachers College Press.

Settles, I. H., Buchanan, N. T., & Dotson, K. (2018). Scrutinized but not recognized: (In)visibility and hypervisibility experiences of faculty of color. *Journal of Vocational Behavior, 113,* 62–74.

Shafir, R. Z. (2003). *The Zen of listening: Mindful communication in the age of distraction.* Quest Books.

Shalaby, C. (2017). *Troublemakers: Lessons in freedom from young children at school.* The New Press.

Siegel, D. J., & Bryson, T. P. (2016). *No-drama discipline: The whole-brain way to calm the chaos and nurture your child's developing mind.* Bantam Books.

Singleton, G. E. (2012). *Courageous conversations about race: A field guide for achieving equity in schools.* Corwin.

Skloot, R. (2017). *The immortal life of Henrietta Lacks.* Broadway Paperbacks.

Smith, A. (2007). Children and young people's participation rights in education. *The International Journal of Children's Rights, 15*(1), 147–164.

Smolcic, E., & Katunich, J. (2017). Teachers crossing borders: A review of the research into cultural immersion field experience for teachers. *Teaching and Teacher Education, 62,* 47–59.

Snow, M. (2015). Little free libraries: A call for research into the tiny book depositories. *Children and Libraries, 13*(4), 30–32.

Song, S., & Swearer, S. M. (2016). The cart before the horse: The challenge and promise of restorative justice consultation in schools. *Journal of Educational and Psychological Consultation, 26*(4), 313–324.

Southern Poverty Law Center. (2016). *Social justice standards: The teaching tolerance anti-bias framework.* Teaching Tolerance. https://www.tolerance.org/frameworks/social-justice-standards

Southern Poverty Law Center. (2019). *The march continues: Five essential practices for teaching the civil rights movement.* Teaching Tolerance. https://www.tolerance.org/sites/default/files/2017-06/March_Continues_Five_Essential_Practices.pdf

Stenner, K. (2005). *The authoritarian dynamic.* Cambridge University Press.

Stewart, M. C., & Arnold, C. L. (2018). Defining social listening: Recognizing an emerging dimension of listening. *International Journal of Listening, 32*(2), 85–100.

Stoughton, E. (2006). Marcus and Harriet: Living on the edge in school and society. In E. A. Brantlinger (Ed.), *Who benefits from special education? Remediating (fixing) other people's children* (pp. 145–163). Erlbaum.

Strauss, D., & Powell, S. (2015). Human rights and children's rights. In T. David, K. Goouch, & S. Powell (Eds.), *The Routledge international handbook of philosophies and theories of early childhood education and care* (pp. 179–188). Routledge.

Stubbs, M. (2002). Some basic sociolinguistic concepts. In L. Delpit (Ed.), *The skin that we speak* (pp. 63–85). The New Press.

Styslinger, M. E. (2017). *Workshopping the canon*. National Council of Teachers of English.

Tanner, S. J. (2019). Whiteness is a white problem: Whiteness in English Education. *English Education, 51*(2), 182–199.

Tatum, A. W. (2006). Engaging African American males in reading. *Educational Leadership, 63*(5), 44.

Tatum, A. (2008). Toward a more anatomically complete model of literacy instruction: A focus on African American male adolescents and texts. *Harvard Educational Review, 78*(1), 155–180.

Tatum, B. D. (2017). *Why are all the Black kids sitting together in the cafeteria? And other conversations about race*. Basic Books.

Taylor, D., & Dorsey-Gaines, C. (1988). *Growing up literate: Learning from inner-city families*. Heinemann.

Thomas, A. (2017). *The hate u give*. Balzer & Bray.

Torres, C. (2018, August 31). "An innate sense of justice": Social justice for small humans. *Education Week*. https://blogs.edweek.org/teachers/intersection-culture -and-race-in-education/2018/08/an-innate-sense-of-justice-picture-books-for -small-humans.html?cmp=soc-twitter-shr

Tovani, C. (2016). The power of purposeful reading. In M. Scherer (Ed.), *On developing readers: Readings from* Educational Leadership (pp. 121–128). Association for Supervision and Curriculum Development.

Trelease, J. (2006). *The read-aloud handbook*. Penguin.

Tyson, K. (2013). Tracking segregation, and the opportunity gap. In P. L. Carter & K. G. Welner (Eds.), *Closing the opportunity gap: What America must do to give every child an even chance* (pp. 169–180). Oxford University Press.

United Nations. (1989, November 20). *Convention on the rights of the child*. https:// www.ohchr.org/en/professionalinterest/pages/crc.aspx

United Nations. (1992, December 18). *Declaration on the rights of persons belonging to national or ethnic, religious and linguistic minorities*. https://www.ohchr .org/Documents/Publications/GuideMinoritiesDeclarationen.pdf

United Nations. (2006). *Handbook on restorative justice programmes*. https://www. unodc.org/pdf/criminal_justice/Handbook_on_Restorative_Justice_Programmes. pdf

Utt, J. (2018). A case for decentering whiteness in education: How Eurocentric social studies curriculum acts as a form of white/western studies. *Ethnic Studies Review, 41*(1–2), 19–34.

Van Ness, D. W. (2012). Creating restorative systems. In L. Walgrave (Ed.), *Restorative justice and the law* (pp. 150–169). Willan.

Van Ness, D., & Strong, K. H. (2010). A brief history of restorative justice: The development of a new pattern of thinking. In D. Van Ness & K. H. Strong (Eds.), *Restoring justice: An introduction to restorative justice* (pp. 21–58). Routledge.

Vaughn, M., Premo, J., Sotirovska, V. V., & Erickson, D. (2020). Evaluating agency in literacy using the student agency profile. *The Reading Teacher, 73*(4), 427–441.

Venezky, R. L., Wagner, D. A., & Ciliberti, B. S. (1990). *Toward defining literacy*. International Reading Association.

Wachtel, T. (2013). *Defining restorative*. International Institute for Restorative Practices. https://www.iirp.edu/restorative-practices/defining-restorative/

Waddell, J. H. (2013). Communities as critical partners in teacher education: The impact of community immersion on teacher candidates' understanding of self and teaching in urban schools. *Current Issues in Education, 16*(2), 1–16.

Walmsley, S. A., & Allington, R. L. (2007). Redefining and reforming instructional support programs for at-risk students. In R. L. Allington & S. A. Walmsley (Eds.), *No quick fix, the RTI edition: Rethinking literacy programs in America's elementary schools* (pp. 19–29). International Reading Association.

Welner, K. G., & Carter, P. L. (2013). Achievement gaps arise from opportunity gaps. In P. L. Carter & K. G. Welner (Eds.), *Closing the opportunity gap: What America must do to give every child an even chance* (pp. 1–10). Oxford University Press.

Wheatley, M. J. (2010). *Finding our way: Leadership for an uncertain time*. Berrett-Koehler.

Wiley, T. G. (2014). Diversity, super-diversity, and monolingual language ideology in the United States: Tolerance or intolerance? *Review of Research in Education, 38*(1), 1–32.

Wiley, T. G., Garcia, D. R., Danzig, A. B., & Stigler, M. L. (2014). Language policy, politics, and diversity in education. *Review of Research in Education, 38*(1), vii–xxiii.

Wilhelm, J. D. (2016). *"You gotta BE the book!" Teaching engaged and reflective reading with adolescents* (3rd ed.). Teachers College Press.

Williams, B. T. (2017). *Literacy practices and perceptions of agency: Composing identities*. Taylor & Francis.

Willingham, D. T. (2017). *The reading mind: A cognitive approach to understanding how the mind reads*. Wiley.

Wingate, U. (2015). *Academic literacy and student diversity: The case for inclusive practice*. Multilingual Matters.

Winn, M. T. (2013). Toward a restorative English education. *Research in the Teaching of English, 48*(1), 126–135.

Winn, M. T. (2018). *Justice on both sides: Transforming education through restorative justice*. Harvard Education Press.

Winn, M., Graham, H., & Renjitham Alfred, R. (2019). *Restorative justice in the English language arts classroom*. National Council of Teachers of English.

Wojtowicz, L. (2018). *Crossing the hall: Exposing an American divide*. Author House.

Wolbring, G. (2008). The politics of ableism. *Development, 51*(2), 252–258.

Wolter, D. L. (2015). *Reading upside down: Identifying and addressing opportunity gaps in literacy instruction*. Teachers College Press.

Wolter, D. L. (2017). Moving readers from struggling to proficient. *Phi Delta Kappan, 99*(1), 37–39.

Wolter, D. L. (2018). *Ears, eyes, and hands: Reflections on language, literacy, and linguistics*. Gallaudet University Press.

Wolvin, A. D., & Cohen, S. D. (2012). An inventory of listening competency dimensions. *International Journal of Listening, 26*(2), 64–66.

Wright, B. L., & Counsell, S. L. (2018). *The brilliance of black boys: Cultivating school success in the early grades*. Teachers College Press.

Zapata, A., Kleekamp, M., & King, C. (2018). *Expanding the canon: How diverse literature can transform literacy learning* [Literacy leadership brief]. International Literacy Association.

Zehr, H. (1990). *Changing lenses: A new focus for crime and justice*. Herald Press.

Zehr, H. (2015). *The little book of restorative justice* (Rev. ed.). Skyhorse.

Index

About the Author

Deborah L. Wolter is a retired literacy consultant for Student Intervention and Support Services in the Ann Arbor (Michigan) Public Schools. She has worked for over 20 years with public school teachers and their students from all walks of life (including those in special education, Title I, and response to intervention, and those who were English language learners) and in different places of exploring multiple languages, literacies, and linguistics. Prior to that, she worked as an early childhood education teacher for 10 years. Deborah completed a BA degree in early childhood and elementary education and an MA degree in reading from Eastern Michigan University. She also completed an additional endorsement in learning disabilities from Madonna University. Deborah has written several papers on literacy and family literacy for professional journals. *Restorative Literacies*, co-published by Teachers College Press and the International Institute for Restorative Practices, is her third book. She is the author of *Reading Upside Down: Identifying and Addressing Opportunity Gaps in Literacy Instruction*, published by Teachers College Press in June 2015. Being deaf since birth, she also offers a unique insider's perspective on opportunity gaps. Her second book, *Ears, Eyes, and Hands: Reflections on Language, Literacy, and Linguistics*, published by Gallaudet University Press, was released in December 2018. A future memoir, *A Search for Stories*, is currently in the works.